T0209626

AuthorHouse™
1663 Liberty Drive
Bloomington, IN 47403
www.authorhouse.com
Phone: 1 (800) 839-8640

Published by AuthorHouse 04/14/2020

ISBN: 978-1-7283-3490-5 (sc)
ISBN: 978-1-7283-3488-2 (hc)
ISBN: 978-1-7283-3489-9 (e)

Library of Congress Control Number: 2019918208

Print information available on the last page.

This book is printed on acid-free paper.

REAL ANSWERS TO

31

MONEY QUESTIONS

THAT KEEP SMALL BUSINESS OWNERS

UP AT NIGHT

MIKE WOLF

authorHOUSE®

This publication contains the opinions and ideas of its author. It is intended to provide helpful and informative material on the subjects addressed in the publication. The author and publisher specifically disclaim all responsibility for any liability, loss, or risk, personal or otherwise, which is incurred as a consequence, directly or indirectly, of the use and application of any of the contents of this book.

WRITERS REPUBLIC L.L.C.
515 Summit Ave. Unit R1
Union City, NJ 07087, USA

Website: *www.writersrepublic.com*
Hotline: *1-877-656-6838*
Email: *info@writersrepublic.com*

Ordering Information:
Quantity sales. Special discounts are available on quantity purchases by corporations, associations, and others. For details, contact the publisher at the address above.

Library of Congress Control Number:	IN-PROCESS	
ISBN-13:	978-1-64620-104-4	[Paperback Edition]
	978-1-64620-105-1	[Hardback Edition]
	978-1-64620-108-2	[Digital Edition]

Rev. date: 04/09/2020

NO TIME FOR HARVARD? NO SWEAT!

KANKETA™

This isn't just another approach to traditional financial management. Kanketa is an eastern based business management philosophy that has been proven over decades. The Kanketa Balanced Budget is a uniquely formed, highly crafted, proven method. It will give you all the day-to-day financial strategies that you will need for the rest of your professional career regardless of where your business takes you.

**ALL THE FINANCE YOU'LL EVER NEED
TO RUN A PROFITABLE SMALL BUSINESS**

<u>GUARANTEED!</u>

My sincerest gratitude

to the 72 executives
of global companies
for your time, energy, effort,
tireless passion and commitment
to helping me form and prove
these concepts

And ...

to all Business Leaders
who are hungry for knowledge,
humble enough to explore change,
smart enough to recognize
and take advantage of
the proven practices of others,
and courageous enough to implement them

I am eternally grateful.

CONTENTS

Every business problem that exists, or has ever existed
is the result of one area of a company
out of balance with another.

All solutions can be found by
putting the company into balance with itself.

Balance internally, and the external forces will follow.
Balance the company, and you will solve the problem.

Mike Wolf

PREFACE

This is a book about money. Your money. The money that runs your small business every day. It is also a book for passionate, skillful people who might be uncomfortable with money talk. I want you to know upfront that this information will require a desire to grow and the willingness to make changes. There is one thing I know for certain. Real success begins at the end of your comfort zone.

My goal is to change how you think about the money in your business. I do not want you to have sleepless nights worrying about payroll like I did in my companies. I want all the guesswork that might be creating errors and costing you time and money to disappear. I want you to be able to add more time and enjoyment to your day. The more you can streamline your finances, the more freedom you will have to do what you do best – and with less stress. I want you to always have enough money to keep your business healthy and growing. You will work less and earn more by touching money only two hours a month, while your financial system runs itself.

My vision is that

> SOMEDAY,
>> all owners of small businesses will
>> manage their companies passionately,
>> in an error-free environment
>> without the stress, mystery and guesswork
>> associated with business finance

This information is different. Very different.

I guarantee that you will not find the information in this book anywhere else. It is not taught in the most expensive business schools. It is not learned on the job. It is not passed down from others. It was gleaned from over a half century of working with global corporations. No single company provided all the material. Over 300 companies each contributed their fair share. Seventy-two global companies stepped up to the plate and went the distance to help me to prove the outcomes.

The results of achieving financial balance come quickly. The concepts are easy to understand and can be immediately used with surprising results. To ensure that you will never be left hanging or wondering, I have included a support phone number in the final pages of this book for you to call, at no cost, with any questions. Additionally, I will make certain tools available to you, again at no cost. My goal is knowledge transfer. This information can change the world.

The secret to a successful business is balance. The Kanketa Balanced Budget is your vehicle to get you there. I will give you a roadmap to follow. The answer is in how you think about money.

GET THE MOST OUT OF THIS BOOK.

There appears to be a lot of detail in these pages. Whatever you do, please don't sweat the details! They will come over time.

Every chapter has the main points that you need to know. Keep to the overview.

The best overview is the Table of Contents. Also, look at the call-out boxes along the way for applied practices. Above all, be courageous. This is a uniquely formed, different approach to financial management. It is a proven prescription for success. If you decide to put these practices to work in your business, I promise that you will reap rewards exponentially.

The good news is that you don't have to do everything all at once to enjoy the benefits. Do what is comfortable first. Dip your toe in or go for a splash. Feel confident knowing that whatever you do is bringing you closer to becoming a high-performing company.

These pages deliver concise answers to the following 31 questions that continue to plague the minds of small business owners.

CHAPTER 1:

NUMBERS DON'T LIE.

Men lie. Women lie. Kids lie. Numbers don't. But, looking at your financial statements, how would you ever know? It's not the numbers that are lying to small business owners. It's small business owners who are lying to the numbers.

"I THINK this month will turn out ok."

"It SEEMS like we are growing."

"It FEELS like we'll have a good year."

"I THINK we're profitable."

"I HOPE we can afford it."

"We'll PROBABLY end up ahead of last year."

Think? Feel? Hope? Pray? Maybe? Probably? These aren't the words of a confident business owner of a safe, high performing company.

Every concept presented here will be reduced to a number that produces specific, quantifiable, reliably predictable results. This is what the Kanketa system puts in place. Nothing more. Nothing less. What you do with the results is up to you.

THE 30 DAY COMPANY

The Kanketa method isolates and manages a business one month at a time. The previous month is history. The coming month hasn't happened yet.

Think of it like this. Your business restarts at midnight on the first day of every month and ends at 11:59 pm. on the last day of the month. During that time you have either made or lost money. A year is twelve 30-day opportunities to win or lose. Last month's P&L is a worthless, uncontrollable slice of history. Everything outside of the immediate 30-day performance cycle is irrelevant. There is nothing else.

THE PROBLEM WITH GAAP ACCOUNTING

> "Death and Taxes have merged.
> My financial statements show a profit.
> Why isn't it in my checking account?"

You instinctively know that you're not managing money as well as you should. You just can't quite put your finger on the problem. Meanwhile, your accountant is mumbling gibberish.

"framistans kj skjfhskj debt to income jhkj snerbs and Retained Earnings for the last fiscal year finorng and that's not a good return on investment snibit, snibit .... so pay these taxes next week, or else!"

We, in the U.S.A., are subject to something called GAAP accounting (Generally Accepted Accounting Principles). Unfortunately, GAAP leaves a big GAP in how business owners think about money. GAAP was invented for the convenience of the IRS, but it is almost useless for small business decision-making. The financial statements provided to you by your accountant are created for tax-compliance purposes. Certainly, this is efficiency is necessary for the stability of our country and its economy. GAAP provides an easy, organized reporting format to the government. But GAAP financial statements are not good business planning tools.

The expense categories in the GAAP system are usually arranged alphabetically according to expense types: **A**dvertising, **B**ank fees, **C**leaning service, **D**elivery, etc. Alphabetical order might help the IRS to process taxes more efficiently, but it is almost useless for helping small business owners make good day-to-day decisions.

GAAP accounting rules demand the exact same accounting procedures for Larry's Landscaping and Garden Supply, a small family-owned business, as they do for IBM, General Motors, Coca Cola and the rest. It must be remembered that certified public accountants are contracted by, and work for the Federal Government. It says so right in their license to practice. They are sworn to uphold government tax laws and protect government interests.

No one wants to be non-compliant and get in trouble with the IRS. Believing they are avoiding trouble, many small business owners completely turn their books over to some accountant to take care of everything. No questions asked.

Accountants do not hold pixie dust and are not a golden guarantee that you will avoid IRS trouble. Your accountant is your first-pass proofreader of your tax situation before you enter the lion's den.

THREE FINANCIAL TOOLS THAT THE GOVERNMENT AND BANKS USE

There are three fundamental financial tools used for business decision-making:

- *Profit and Loss Statement (P&L) tells **how much** money you made*

- *Balance Sheet tells you **where** your money is*

- *Cash Flow Statement tells you **when** you can spend it*

Reading Financial Statements

Most small business entrepreneuers haven't attended business school and they rely on monthly P&L statements (and in some cases fortune cookies) to answer their business questions.

I often hear comments like "we are ahead of last year at this time" or "our utilities costs are down over last year."

Think of all the changes that happen to a company in just one year that impact tour finances and your P&L statement. Social changes, technological, economic, environmental, political, legal, ethical, and demographic changes in age, education and income. Now add the changes in personnel, and ownership changes within your customers' and your vendors' businesses, and in your own business, not to mention the priority changes that show up in your personal life.

What possible relevance or meaningful value does a comparison to the previous year have?

Recently, there was a business advisor as a guest and speaker on a national television show who stated that a small business should focus on its balance sheet, not on its sales. His compelling presentation was well received by the audience.

Yes, the speaker is generally correct about eyes on the balance sheet; what you own and what you owe. However, in the context of his presentation, it would be like a medical doctor who is prescribing an aspirin for cancer. A balance sheet is a symptom of good financial management, but in my opinion, it is not a critical component of everyday business decision-making. The person who focuses on a balance sheet would have a different agenda than the day-to-day management of a business, such as getting a loan, selling or leasing the company, or making purchases that strengthen the company's value.

The P&L statement is the barometer for how much money you are making. The balance sheet is your month end snapshot-in-time that tells you where your money is at the moment. A cash flow statement tells you when you can spend it. Accurate and diligent day-to-day budget management will control the outcome of the balance sheet and the cash flow statement, but not the other way around. It will be your ability to adhere to a budget that underlies the success of your business.

I say, get some sleep, lower your stress level and watch your headache disappear. Take an aspirin to tie you over until bedtime.

On the following page is a simple example of a GAAP P&L. I chose this very simple example of a Start-Up company over a more complex version because it graphically illustrates how the smallest of Start-Up businesses typically spring out of the gate. An annual revenue of $50,000 or less is a hobby.

This example is a typical Kodak moment as a business moves off the launchpad. Notice the alphabetical arrangement of expenses.

Alphabet Soup – The GAAP P&L

Larry's Landscaping & Garden Supply
Profit & Loss
October 2011 through September 2012

	Oct '11 - Sep 12
Ordinary Income/Expense	
Income	
Landscaping Services	57,860.36
Markup Income	815.00
Retail Sales	383.03
Service	6,640.00
Total Income	65,698.39
Cost of Goods Sold	
Cost of Goods Sold	4,220.25
Total COGS	4,220.25
Gross Profit	61,478.14
Expense	
Payroll Expenses	37,820.65
Automobile	738.05
Bank Service Charges	73.50
Delivery Fee	15.00
Insurance	1,835.00
Interest Expense	470.91
Job Expenses	2,427.25
Mileage Reimbursement	0.00
Professional Fees	375.00
Rent	2,400.00
Repairs	45.00
Tools and Misc. Equipment	735.00
Uncategorized Expenses	0.00
Utilities	655.55
Total Expense	47,590.91
Net Ordinary Income	13,887.23
Other Income/Expense	
Other Income	
Misc Income	762.50
Interest Income	91.11
Total Other Income	853.61
Net Other Income	853.61
Net Income	14,740.84

I find that owners of small companies usually base most of their decisions on three numbers: sales, Net Profit and Gross Profit, in that order.

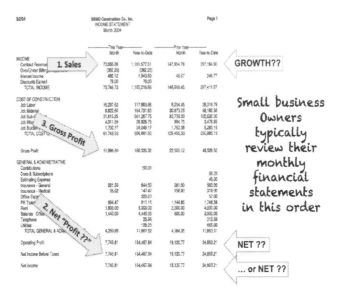

Typically, owners review their Profit and Loss statements (P&Ls are historical data) by first looking at the Gross Sales for last month. Next, their eyes anxiously skip to the "bottom line" profit. Finally, they might quickly glance at the Gross Profit.

Profit, profit, profit! The definition of the word "profit" is so often confused and there seems to be as many different definitions of profit as the number of People you ask. Kanketa substitutes the word "MARGIN" for Gross Profit.

In truth, it really doesn't matter much whether the numbers in the financial statements are overlooked, because they don't offer a sense of how the business is actually performing.

In this GAAP P&L, the business owner, upon seeing the bottom line, is certainly having a joyful day. "Ah ... It shows a nice Net Profit" comes Larry's shout of sheer delight. Larry might quickly gloss over the Gross Profit in the process. But he is so relieved with the good bottom line news, that he is all too happy to pay the accountant the $250 for the month before he tosses the statement into the bottom drawer, never again to be looked at.

With a gleeful heart he yells up the stairs to his wife; "Hey Sylvia, we made some money this month. We can buy the boat!"

It doesn't take long for Sylvia to reply. "Honey, it's great that we made a good profit, but I hate to tell you that there is only $300 in the business account and we need it for groceries."

Most small companies calculate the success of the game by counting ticket sales. They focus on their P&L Net Profit instead of focusing on improving attendance by using their on-the-field playbook. Smart coaches know that If the proven playbook is diligently observed, ticket sales will follow. When revenue on the P&L is not in the checkbook, a good coach won't obsess about the uncontrollable factors in the marketplace. They focus on what can be controlled.

When money for payroll is not in the checkbook,
when money for expenses to run the business is not in the checkbook,
when the Net Profit showing on the P&L is not in the checkbook,
fix the current money management process, and don't lose sleep over last month's underperformance that caused this month's problem.

Q: So... what's the point of P&Ls?

A: Preparing to report taxes that aren't due yet.

If you take a minute to search the web for examples of Profit and Loss statements, you will literally find thousands of every type of P&L in existence. As you give attention to the main differences between P&Ls you will notice items listed as job costs (Cost of Goods Sold). You will see operating overhead costs of every description. Yet, not one of those thousands of statements remotely identifies, suggests or offers real solutions to problems in a business.

> **GAAP accounting is for tax-paying purposes.**
> **GAAP is not a good day-to-day**
> **decision-making tool for business.**

I will offer a better way to think about and manage your finances. A much better way.

The Kanketa Balanced Budget

I am promoting the concept of a Balanced Budget. A Balanced Budget will create short and long term safety for any company during economic swings, as I am about to show you. One of the 12 guiding principles of Kanketa is "Safety first. Profit second."

> The Kanketa Balanced Budget is a monetary structure
> of 10 critical performance components
> that applies to every business on the planet.
> A Balanced Budget is a protection
> against unforeseen change.

I hired an outside research firm to use Google, Bing and many search engines to find anything close to the Balanced Budgeting practices that I will present here. The research yielded no results of any value. If you search all day long, chances are excellent that you will come up empty-handed with the concepts of financial balance that you will learn in this book.

Balanced Budgeting is held close to the vest and is almost exclusively practiced at the top of large global companies (and even then, not with great efficiency). It is almost never seen in a company of less than a couple thousand people. Why is this important? Balanced Budgeting is what makes big companies big. I know this firsthand. I learned this over decades from the best of them. These practices work just as well in small companies of 1 to 30 employees as you will see.

It is important to understand that accountants play a big part in balancing budgets. Their contributions are different than their traditional GAAP training teaches. They are not the final word, but they certainly can be significant collaborators on the financial team of a business.

"Why this? My accountant takes care of everything."

Business Advisor or Accountant?

There's more to accounting than a good accountant. This is why you must become a student of your business. After all, it's the business that promises to support your family and carry you for years. At the very least, learn some sound basics.

Stay in control of your money. Don't just blindly hand it all to an accountant or to anyone for any reason and assume you are in good hands. This isn't an Allstate commercial. Above all, don't rely on your accountant to walk you through life. He can't, and she won't.

This perspective might help.

BUSINESS ADVISOR OR ACCOUNTANT? BATMAN OR ROBIN?

Imagine what would happen if all of the villains attacked Gotham City.

The police are losing the battle. The city is in complete turmoil. People everywhere are being dropped in vats of green goo and all the banks are being held for ransom by the Joker and the Penguin.

Then the searchlight goes up and hovers over the tall buildings, calling on our heroes for help. But, lo and behold, it is a silhouette of Robin. As the crowds of angry people gather outside of the mayor's office demanding answers, the mayor steps forward with an announcement.

"Friends of Gotham, this year, Robin has the contract. He only charges a small monthly retainer and he's been reasonably reliable. Seems to always show up on time. His outfits are clean and in good shape. Granted, he doesn't have the Batmobile, but my office was able to get him a great lease deal on a new Toyota Camry. And, hey, we do trust him. He understands the villains' rules, and was sufficiently trained to at least scale the main walls of the important buildings around town. He has good English, keeps good records, and I'm sure he can represent us well to the Joker."

Batman

- ✓ THE FUNNEL - pours the splash
- ✓ BIG PICTURE
- ✓ The SHOE...
- ✓ MAIN CATEGORIES
- ✓ BIG SWIPES
- ✓ CREATES BALANCE
- ✓ DESIGNS, DEVELOPS, IMPLEMENTS BALANCE
- ✓ PROACTIVE
- ✓ MONTHLY REPORTS
- ✓ LEAD – Front end
- ✓ QUANTIFIES
- ✓ BUDGET, SCORECARD

Robin

- ✓ THE SPOUT - channels the drips
- ✓ DETAILS, REFINEMENT
- ✓ ... The LACES
- ✓ SUB-CATEGORIES
- ✓ TRIM and CLEAN UP
- ✓ MAINTAINS BALANCE
- ✓ MANAGES BALANCE
- ✓ AVOIDS REACTIVE
- ✓ QUARTERLY REPORTS
- ✓ FOLLOW – Back end
- ✓ VERIFIES
- ✓ P&L, BALANCE SHEET

If you want your business to be more than a hobby, you will need both an accountant and a business advisor. They could be two-in one. Get control of your business, or someone else will.

> The job of a business advisor is to help <u>design</u> and <u>develop</u> the big picture and create balance in the business.
> The job of an accountant is to help <u>manage</u> the details and <u>maintain</u> the balance.
> Successful businesses have both.

True Story: My Accountant Takes Care of Everything

Barry F. of Scranton, Penn. was happy with his accounting services. His accountant took care of everything – balanced the books, saved the receipts, organized the tax records – the whole shebang. This allowed Barry to focus on his tool and die shop worry free. After all, his accountant took care of everything. All the books, all the receipts. all the taxes. Barry was in very good hands.

One day Barry received a distressing call that his accountant just passed away.

Barry, who hadn't looked at his books for five years, had no idea where to begin. He knew he needed to find any accountant fast. Despite an exhaustive search, Barry was unable to find an accountant with the same with dedication and total service. In despair, Barry began to tackle the books himself.

Barry used his QuickBooks as his bible. His problems grew in proportion to the bookkeeping entry errors he made. He treated whatever ended up at the bottom line of his financial statement as his checkbook balance. Barry spent profits that didn't exist.

He managed to keep a shoebox full of receipts, many of which were non-deductible.

It wasn't long before Barry's checkbook was completely empty, and so was his shop. No employees. No equipment. At least there were no more tool and die worries at his new job at UPS.

CHAPTER 2:

FOLLOWING THE KANKETA MONEY MAP

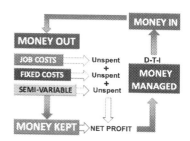

What is the Kanketa Money Map?

You can't lead your company from behind. Following the Kanketa Money Map keeps you on course and ensures that your Balanced Budget arrives at your destination on time. The Money Map is a straightforward set of instructions, created by folks who have made the trip before.

The Money Map shows you a convenient, comfortable ride. Your Money Map has a specific starting point, a "snapshot in time." There is a route to follow. Your financial journey begins at midnight on the first day of every month. Your arrival time is scheduled for midnight on the last day of the month. You either win, or you lose.

Wash. Rinse. Repeat.

As with any map, you will encounter cracks in the road and detours. You will travel over hills, plains and valleys. There will be caution signs and stop signs to observe that will slow you down, but keep you safe. Your Money Map landscape has four connecting lanes:

MONEY IN
MONEY OUT
MONEY KEPT
MONEY MANAGED

THE MONEY MAP BEGINS WITH A BALANCED BUDGET

Your financial journey must follow the road in a specific sequence of events. If you travel on a train, and it makes a 10- minute station stop, you can't wander off to sniff the buttercups in the meadow or you might not get back to the train on time. If your car reverses and you drive against traffic, your trip will become unsafe.

As you are packing for your trip, begin with the end in mind. If you don't know where you're going, any road will take you there.

Before putting the key into the ignition, it is necessary to be sure that your vehicle is in good working order. A Balanced Budget is your vehicle that promises a safe, comfortable ride. The Balanced Budget is needed to make the entire Money Map work.

The Balance Budget is the roadmap on a universal landscape that never changes. It will be necessary to consider the size of your business. The Kanketa Balanced Budget is clearly marked along the way and works exactly the same for Amazon, Google, McDonalds, Coca Cola, as it does for Larry's Landscaping & Garden Supply, and as it will work for your business. The only difference is the business size. Size can slow you down or speed you up, but the results are proportionately the same. Having said this, your Money Map will serve you nicely for the rest of your professional career. In this book I will show you how to set up the financial picture for your small company and view it in the same way as many global corporations do.

> **An efficient business is managed 30 days at a time. Last month was history. Next month hasn't happened yet. In the current 30 days, you either made or lost money. Repeat 12 times in a row for an annual result**

Business size answers questions like, "How much could, would, should my business pay me every month for the work I do?"

Your size depends upon on why and how you pay yourself. You will make a salary as an employee of your company. Maybe you will charge your company rent for a building you own or a loan that you give to your company. Hopefully, you will make a profit as the owner of your company. In the Money Map, you will see how business owners are paid along with everyone else and do not have to be paid last. Everything follows a simple set of rules in a specific sequence.

TEN PARTS OF THE KANKETA BALANCED BUDGET

There are 10 key components to manage in the Kanketa Balanced Budget. Here's the good news! In a Balanced Budget, your money is always in the checkbook. Each of the four main parcels in the Money Map has its own unique terrain.
Your Money Map has 10 touch points.

Money In
1. Gross Sales
2. Net Sales
3. Cost of Quality

Money Out
4. Cost of Goods Sold
5. Fixed Costs
6. Semi-Variable Costs

Money Kept
7. Reinvestment
8. Retained Earnings

Money Managed
9. Taxes
10. Shareholders

The goal is to create balance within these categories.

A COMPANY OF ONE

"How does this apply to me if I'm a company of one?"

"Sure, I would like to grow my business, and maybe have an employee or two. But, this is a lot of work for little old me. I'm still at the starting gate." You are already doing a lot of work. Believe me when I say that if you plan to be a company of one, you have job, not a company. No one will buy it or lease it from you, because there is nothing to buy or lease. But, if you have the desire to grow, and have the willingness to make changes, this information will definitely help you.

One is the loneliest number

You might be old enough to remember the hit song by the band Three Dog Night, "One is the loneliest number (that ya' ever knew)." This is especially true in a small business. The owner of a company of one must market, sell, conduct customer service and be sure that customers don't leave. When she is not doing these things, she is creating products, dealing with suppliers, attending to operational responsibilities and doing bookkeeping.

The workload of a business is in proportion to the number of managers available. In a company of two people, the workload is cut in half. What doesn't go away or get dissected are the eight equal and inseparable functions of every company on the planet: product management, production, delivery, human resource development, marketing, sales, customer service, and customer care. None of these can be ignored or the rest become crippled.

Kanketa principles apply to a company of one, a hundred or a million. A Kanketa Balanced Budget does not require a business to be a certain size, or to be in full bloom in order to have the benefits of this information. The only requirement is that whoever is leading the company must have the desire to grow the business, be willing to make the necessary changes, and be diligent about managing money for at least two hours a week.

> All Kanketa practices universally apply to any business size or type. A company of one, or a company of 100,000. The difference isn't the size of the business, but the size of the owner's desire to grow and their willingness to change.

True Story: A Company of One

Libby H. in Austin, Texas was the sole proprietor of a dog kennel business. For 12 years, she earned a reasonable living and paid her bills on time. When her mother became ill, Libby closed her kennel to give her mother full time home care.

In choosing to provide home care, Libby fulfilled her role as a devoted daughter.

Unfortunately, Libby didn't realize that keeping her business running and caring for her mother wasn't a binary choice. With just one or two employees and a system that could run the company in her absence, Libby would have received a full time income while taking care of her mother, and she would have been able to return to work at some point in the future while the business continued to grow without her.

I calculated that Libby lost $372,000 by assuming that her company of one was only as big as her mind's eye. The moral of the story: Don't make assumptions about the value of your business based on what you hear from others or what might seem to be the obvious decisions to make. It costs nothing to ask.

Your findings might surprise you.

THE BALANCING ACT

Financial Balance is an eastern business discipline that is mostly practiced in Asia. I have generally found that American small businesses are less disciplined about following budgets than business owners of other countries.

The Kanketa Balanced Budget is dynamic, holistic, and leaves nothing out. It is often called a "transitional budget" because the expenses and the Net Profit move and breathe in balance with the sales performance of the business.

I will say with supreme confidence that 99% of all small U.S. business owners do not strive for, or even know about Balanced Budgeting. If they did, more business coaches would teach it and I believe that the current U.S. 85% failure rate for small business Start-Ups could be reduced by two-thirds within the first five years.

It is unfortunate that the internet is swarming with unverifiable, unproven, conflicting and confusing ideas about money and management, sold by many self-appointed people with unfounded experience. Add to these detours are what is not taught in our business schools and universities. The roots of U.S. business management in the world market are steadily eroding with each new generation. The blind are leading the blind.

Whether or not you own a business, or are managing one for someone else, there are two factors that should always be considered with every decision you make:

- *Financial balance is essential to building stability, safety and growth.*
- *The impact of every decision you make will bring you closer to or drive you away from a point of balance.*

Kanketa defines Financial Balance as...

the point in the Margin
at which Fixed overhead costs,
Semi-Variable overhead costs,
and Net Profit are equal.

Financial balance is created from
all money of a business,
repositioned differently.

Kanketa defines Normal as ...

An ideal monthly performance level, based on
the 12-month average of income and expenses
from the previous tax year, at which
all resources of the company are fully utilized.

Normal is the center of a business's financial universe
and the starting point for company growth.

It sounds complicated at first, but once you see how it works, it's less difficult
than a game of Tic Tac Toe.

> **Normal is the ideal monthly sales performance
> level at which all resources are fully utilized
> without the need for further expense. Normal
> is the starting point
> for the growth of a business.**

TAKING INVENTORY

"What expenses must I budget for?"

Before we begin our Money Map journey, it's always a good idea to stop and take inventory, even when your company is ten and twenty years old.

What are your current resources at hand and what do you still need?

Manpower	Do you have the time to give to your business? Do you have enough of the right kind of help?
Measurements	How will you measure your progress?
Machines	Are you properly equipped? Cellphone? Computers? Vehicles? Other equipment to produce your products and services?
Methods	Do you have standard processes and efficient systems in place?

Most Trusted Partners

Do you have strategic supplier relationships with people who have your best interest in mind and who are willing to understand your business and help you grow it?

Materials	Do you have the supplies needed to meet demand?
Milieu	Do you have sufficient workspace?
Mindset	Do you have the passion, drive and commitment to build and support the vision and mission of your business?
Money	Do you have the funding sources and financial reserves to create the business that is in your mind's eye?

These components will affect the financial balance of your business. It's all about balance.

CHAPTER 3:

BUDGET
SECTION 1 of 10

GROSS SALES

We begin with money in. Kanketa defines Gross Sales as the total amount of money that is <u>deposited</u> into your bank as a result of the sale and production of products and services. Kanketa promotes a cash accounting method, not an accrual accounting method.

After many years of working with thousands of small businesses, I continue to witness general misconceptions about "Gross Sales". You would think that Gross Sales is an accepted standard definition. After all, aren't Gross Sales all the money that comes into the company? No, it isn't. In small businesses, Gross Sales are often mingled with general bank deposits - "miscellaneous income." Guesswork drives accountants cuckoo.

For years, Steve H. of Noblesville, Indiana ran a respectable auto repair business. He was passionate about his work and treated his employees well. Steve loved cars and spent most of his time under the hood. Steve didn't take to bookkeeping, but he didn't trust others to manage his money. He did as little as possible to manage his banking affairs, other than making deposits and signing checks.

Steve had started his business without bank loans. Instead, he took loans from friends and family. In the early 1990's, Steve's business began to grow, and along with it, so did his banking duties. Customer payments were coming in faster than ever, and Steve found himself depositing money every other day.

Steve had a habit of mixing customer payments with loans from friends and family, refunds from customers, credits for product returns and whatever hit the bank. Then, at the end of the month when things slowed down a bit, Steve would glance at his bank statements and, low and behold, marvel at all the deposits, which to Steve, were his total sales for the month.

Every so often I heard Steve would say: "Ooops, yeah, I forgot that Phil paid me a refund." Not only was this a nightmare for Steve's accountant, but these casual habits continued for years. Steve would boast that his shop was doing $500,000 a year, when, in reality he was only selling 80% of this.

Finally, Steve went to get a business loan for expansion. On the application, where it asks, "What are your annual sales?" Steve proudly entered a half million dollars. The bank's underwriters begged to differ because Steve's cashflow only supported a company with $410,000 Gross Sales. Steve was very disappointed with what the bank would lend him.

Fast forward seven years, Steve decided to sell his company. There were several interested buyers. When their accountants pour over Steve's financials, they soon learned that Steve's sales performance was not as represented. The highest bidder was only willing to pay less than half of the asking price for the business. After removing all the irrelevant miscellaneous income in the audit, Steve hobbled away with a disappointing settlement for far less money than he thought his business was worth.

All too often small business managers and owners fail to take the time to clearly, accurately and properly identify and separate their general incoming payments from their sales activity. Many small companies routinely accept and deposit various types of revenue into one general business checking account without properly separating and logging the deposit information. There are many reasons why they do this.

For example: they've loaned money to a key struggling supplier to keep the supplier in business, and as they receive and deposit the supplier's payments, they discover later that they mistakenly recorded the money as Gross Sales. As a result, they might deposit interest payments from a loan they made into the general checking account. They might deposit overpayments and reimbursements from vendors. Maybe it's a loan from family and friends.

There are many different types of deposits that fall under the title of revenue that aren't a sale from products and services. I will use revenue as a general term for all deposits: cash sales, credit card transactions, outside loan repayments - everything that you are paid!

> **Companies too often deposit various types of revenue into one general checking account without properly identifying the revenue.**

Label it to Enable it!

When someone pays you, the payment falls under the title of general revenue (miscellaneous income) until it is clear that you are paid for a specific product or service that you make and or sell. Only then can it be counted as a gross sale. Still, only you know what the money received was for.

When deposits are not clearly labeled, the total Gross Sales picture becomes cloudy, and the important financial details can be inaccurate. It is critical to specifically notate the purpose of every deposit. In the English language, a casually scribbled memo or a missing notation can lead to misinterpretation.

Account Codes

At one point, someone came up with the idea of labeling all the aspects of profit and loss with a set of numbers called "account codes."

By the way, everything here might sound like it's specifically aimed at manufacturing. It isn't. Please know that everything here also equally applies to any service or non-profit business.

It is my experience that small businesses rely too heavily on their accountants to categorize and classify their income and expenses. Your accountant isn't following you around every day. S/he can't sniff out your intentions for your income and expenses.

Without complete information about your company's finances, your accountant must do guesswork to make sense of things. The guesses can be wrong and cost you a lot of money. Failure to provide your accountant with timely, accurate, legible, and complete information can get expensive and lead to unnecessary errors and significant tax expenses.

Why else do you think accountants have those long legal disclaimers on the first page of your financial statements? They are disclaiming their guesses.

THE SALE:
TO BE OR NOT TO BE

What is a "Sale"?

The variety of answers cause large misunderstandings daily in the world's largest of companies. Just because you send someone an invoice, does not necessarily mean that you made a sale.

... A Target

A sale includes a legal agreement to provide a clearly defined value, or a set of deliverables within a specific timeframe, for a specific payment amount.

... A Budget

The payment may be an agreed to amount upon amount of money or "payment in kind", whether the payment is in exchange for things like a trade for services or tangible items, service time, or any other form of equal value.

... A Timeframe

A sale must be delivered within a specified time.

> **In Kanketa, a sale must be fully earned, and is only final when there is nothing more to deliver and no further liability.**

Gross Revenue is Not Necessarily Gross Sales

Gross revenue is all deposits into the company checkbook - sales, revenue, loans, interest revenue, warranty revenue, factoring revenue, etc. However, gross revenue does not necessarily specify which money you earn comes from the sales of your products and services, and later, as memory slips, so does the reason why you were paid. It is crucial to keep income and expenses carefully identified.

At the end of the year, you don't want to have a false sense of how your business performed because your product sales were mixed with unrelated income. Imagine how bitterly disappointed you'd feel if you learned that instead of earning $300,000 from the sales of products and services, you actually only received $230,000 from the services you provided.

When used properly, account codes should add definition, organization and clarity to the sources of your income, and help you to separate the purpose of your income and expenses.

You may use your accountant's codes or use your own. If your accountant is more comfortable with theirs, then, by all means use them.

The account numbers are not as important as the organizational benefits you get from using codes. This formal numbering system is your "Chart of Accounts."

Account codes will help to expose, avoid and remove error, and increase your overall financial accuracy. This helps you to make more money in the short and the long run. In the Kanketa system, the Chart of Accounts will be critical to your financial success as you will learn later in this book.

Right of Rescission

A sale might produce a payment from a customer that may be on deposit, but in many cases, it should not be spent for 72 hours. This gives the customer the right to inspect the delivery of your completed work before they accept your bill. This is called a "right of rescission." By law, you may only spend customer's money up to that portion of your work that has already been satisfactorily completed.

If evidence of any earned income is missing, you have a sale in progress, but you do not legally have a completed sale. Without proof of a specifically defined target, an agreed to monetary exchange or equal value for service and a defined start-end time frame for delivery, chances are excellent that you would lose in a court of law.

Work In Progress: A Kanketa Sale is Earned Income

There is a law in most states that protects the customer from "contractor theft," which is a felony punishable by fines and often, jail time. When you accept and spend customer money for an incomplete job, you may only spend the customer's money in proportion to the work completed.

If you buy materials and supplies for the job, you may spend that portion of the customer's money for the materials and supplies. If you complete 20% of the work, you may only spend 20% of the customer's payment for work that you furnished or satisfactorily delivered. In all cases, you must be able to produce evidence of completion.

Earned Income

Earned income should be the cash you have received from the Gross Sales showing on your P&L statement that you have earned and that you may spend. The key idea here is "proportionate value of all labor, services, and products or materials."

I've seen cases where the judge demanded to see the supplier's checkbook. The contractor's bank balance was lower than the unfinished work that the customer paid for. The supplier was guilty of contractor theft, a felony resulting in restitution and jail time.

When you accept and deposit the customer's payment, spend only that money for which you have evidence of completion and only for the work you have delivered in proportion to the value of all labor, services, products and/or materials.

In a job that has several payments, notify the customer of the work that you have completed. Be sure to identify all income and expenses with account numbers.

Gross income is all money that an individual receives during the year, both as a worker and as an investor.

Earned income is for time and includes only wages, commissions, and bonuses, and business income, minus expenses, if the person is self-employed.

> **You may only spend "earned income" from customer payments that you receive in proportion to the work for which you have evidence of satisfactory completion.**

Money In: Cash or Accrual?

"Accrual" is the accumulation of payments or benefits owed to you by a customer for work that has been completed, but not yet invoiced.

Accrual is an accounting method that records revenues and expenses when they are incurred, regardless of when cash is exchanged.

An invoice is a list of goods sent or services already provided, with a statement of the sum due for these; a bill.

Most small business owners believe that they can spend all money as they want for whatever they want when they receive and deposit it – even if it is intended as a pre-payment, advanced for work to be done. This is not accurate. Many business owners spend money received and intended for one customer to pay for another customer's job. This comingling of funds leaves a grey area for legal dispute – a close cousin to a Ponzi Scheme.

If, by law, fees are earned for the proportionate amount of a job already done – not for work to be done – you may not spend money received that is not yet yours.

Be sure to be able to show recorded evidence that the work specifically invoiced to a customer was satisfactorily completed. If you have no evidence of completion, it is not accrual, and an invoice sent does not yet qualify.

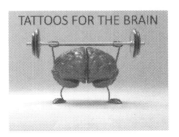

TATTOOS FOR THE BRAIN

THREE GROSS SALE TATTOOS FOR THE BRAIN

Here are three main takeaways for the Gross Sales of a Kanketa Balanced Budget.

#1 A Gross Sale must have a target, a budget (monetary or value exchange) and a time frame to be legally collectible.

#2. A Gross Sale has a Right of Rescission, an allowed time to inspect the product or service before taking possession of it.

#3. You may only spend "earned income" from customer payments that you receive in proportion to the work for which you have evidence of satisfactory completion.

True Story: The Four Sentence E-mail That Cost $30,000

Alex's construction company in southern Wisconsin was hired to do a home remodel. The total of the project was $95,000. The homeowner paid Alex $65,000 toward the job. A shortage of workers delayed Alex by weeks. In the meantime, Alex spent $30,000 on payroll for other work that his company was able to complete during the delay.

The homeowner decided to halt the project and demanded an immediate full refund of the $65,000. Alex claimed that there was $30,000 in completed work. The homeowner took Alex to Court and sued for the full amount. Since Alex could not produce evidence of "earned income," the judge's ruling was contractor theft by Wisconsin law.

A simple email notification by Alex to the homeowner immediately after the $30,000 of work was completed with a detailed description of the work delivered would have prevented the unfavorable outcome. Regardless of the actual work completed, Alex had to repay the full amount with payments over years to avoid a felony charge.

Suggested Email:

Hello (Mr. Homeowner),

On Tuesday, September 16th, 2018, we completed 15% of your total job. We delivered the list of services shown in the attachment. Please inspect this part of the job. If I have not heard otherwise by September 19th, I will assume that this part of the project was to your complete satisfaction.

Thank you for the opportunity to serve you.

NET SALES
AFTER COST OF QUALITY

There are two parts to a sale: Gross Sale and Net Sale.

The Gross Sale is the total amount of money that you expect to receive from producing and/or selling your products and services or for other payments you receive for products or services, such as interest and late fees that you charge.

Cost of Quality

Then there is the "OOPS", the **O**ften **O**verlooked **P**art of the **S**ale which is something called the "Cost of Quality."

Every business has a Cost of Quality. Some of your Cost of Quality might be the discounted costs to deliver to the full satisfaction of your customers. I am putting the Cost of Quality in the "MONEY IN" chapter but the Cost of Quality isn't really "Money In" at all. It's money that was never really yours in the first place. It looks like part of the sale. It might hit your checkbook at one point, but it leaves just as quickly.

On your tax return, the IRS recognizes the Cost of Quality as "returns and allowances." Kanketa sees returns and allowances as more than a few tax items that you can deduct from your taxes for taking a product back or writing off an unpaid customer debt.

Cost of Quality is the total money that might or might not be deposited that you don't get to keep.

Cost of Quality includes your customer discounts that you allow and somehow hope to recapture later.

Cost of Quality is your money for the product and service warranties you stand by - the money that you receive now but will eventually pay out if customers return defective or underperforming products. Warranties are a liability to your company.

Cost of Quality are the costs of your customer freebies; the cost of your samples, free tests, trials and surveys not charged for to get the customer interested. These expenses evaporate and are generally not recovered unless you make an effort to do so.

Cost of Quality are your discounts to employees for products and services. These are your non-charged-for cost of production plus your cost of operating, plus the loss of your profit since you could have sold the products to your customers for full price.

Cost of Quality are your returns and rework because of internal errors.

The bottom line: Cost of Quality are the cost of customer discounts, costs for error and rework, defects or a return of a product that was not delivered as expected, warranties that your customer still might redeemed in the future, restocking costs, free samples that you give away, and customer and vendor errors that you can't get paid for.

Cost of Quality is rarely tracked and often illusive.

Gross Sales are the total collected amount that you invoice before the Cost of Quality
(discounts, rework, returns, samples, free assessments, warranties and error).
Net Sales are the money you keep after all costs of quality have been deducted.

The money left after removing these often overlooked and unaccounted for items is the net sale is what you get to work with.

Net Sales more accurately represent your true sales picture.

Who Pays for Cost of Quality?

Most small business owners call the Cost of Quality a cost of doing business. They don't invest a lot of time or effort trying to recover these costs in view of everything else that needs to be accomplished.

The Kanketa philosophy is you don't always have to win, just never lose. Kanketa sees every loss as critical, regardless of its size. Tiny leaks lead to small losses lead to bigger losses. Loss is not classified in order of importance. Loss is loss.

The Kanketa system recommends budgeting, tracking, monitoring and eventually recovering Cost of Quality. These costs should be built into the price as part of the company's service. If these costs are not recovered, the owner of the business personally pays for Cost of Quality out of the owner's Net Profit.

The money left after removing these often overlooked and unaccounted for items is the Net Sale. The Net Sale is all you get to work with for paying bills and getting to a Net Profit.

Net Sales more accurately represents your true sales picture.

Why Track Cost of Quality?

The Kanketa system tracks the Cost of Quality to get to the Net Sale.

Cost of Quality can be a big number. It can also get out of control quite easily.

The net sale is the actual money you keep after subtracting your Cost of Quality from your gross sale. This is the total amount of money that has been deposited that you have to work with for the job.

I use a "recovery bank" that reminds me to tag recovery charges onto future sales.

I encourage you to clearly define and closely monitor your Cost of Quality and develop a recovery process that is comfortable for you. In any regard, you should budget something for Cost of Quality. If Cost of Quality includes the cost of errors made by your company, then, certainly you are on a mission to avoid and eliminate error. This is all the more reason why it is valuable to monitor, measure and track Cost of Quality.

> **Net Sales, after deducting Cost of Quality, is the amount of money from which the month's budget is established.**

True Story: Discounts Are Paid For By The Owner

Phillip T's Bar-B-Que restaurant in Boston gave discounts to every customer to entice them to return. Phillip allowed 17 employees to eat at half-price. His cooks often made significant kitchen errors. Yet, Phillip freely gave out promotional coupons for every holiday and occasion. He gave generous discounts to the police and government workers. He was more than happy to give discounts to veterans, and to most charity organizations.

Phillip had excellent food, and his revenue grew briskly every year by nearly 30%. Three years later, after his sales had more than doubled, Phillip found himself working harder, and longer to earn the same salary while his company profits steadily dwindled.

Phillip's food was in demand, but his high Cost of Quality had equaled his Net Profit. He found himself working overtime to keep up with his discounts.

Finally, Phillip had to close his doors because he couldn't meet expenses. Phillip's unattended Cost of Quality ate his company for lunch.

> **Discounts and rebates must be planned for and budgeted. If you don't do this, you are expecting the owner to pay for them out of the owner's pocket.**

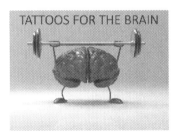

THREE NET SALE TATTOOS FOR THE BRAIN

Here are three main takeaways for the Net Sales of a Kanketa Balanced Budget.

#1 A Net Sale is the amount of money you have to work with after discounts, returns, allowances and error.

#2. A Net Sale, not gross sale, is the primary income number that is used to determine the performance of a business.

#3. A Net Sale is the result of total deposits for products and services, minus the Cost of Quality. The Cost of Quality should be monitored, tracked and be ultimately recoverable in the price of the products and services.

CHAPTER 4:

MONEY OUT

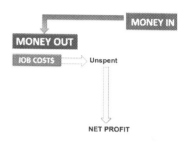

"What should my business expenses be?"

Money Out is the budget for expenses. In the Kanketa Balanced Budget, there is a delicate balancing act for every main type of expense. When a Money Out budget is established, everything that is unspent becomes a contribution to the overall Net Profit of the company.

BUDGET
PART 3 of 10

JOB COSTS
COST OF GOODS SOLD

Job related costs are also known as Cost of Goods Sold. Accountants will sometimes refer to Cost of Goods as "cost of sales." You don't have job costs (Cost of Goods Sold) unless or until you have a job. This makes your job costs dynamic; they are "variable costs" because they vary with the performance of your business.

Cost of Goods Sold Are Classified Under Five General Headings:

1. Direct labor
2. Commissions
3. Contracted services
4. Materials and supplies
5. A category for "all other"

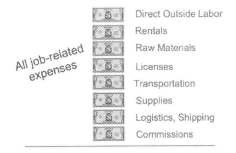

Kanketa loves round numbers in budgets. Kanketa hates round numbers in accounting.

Cost of Goods Sold are needed to create and produce your products and services. Trying to count, track, remember and manage budget numbers that you have little control over is a waste of time. It's a good idea to keep your Cost of Goods budget as a rounded, easy number to remember.

When your business performs at 100% Normal, the budget at 100% should only reflect the Cost of Goods required to produce at that level. Nothing more. Nothing less. In other words, at 100% performance, the business should never need more Cost of Goods to achieve that level of delivery. By ensuring this, the Cost of Goods Sold percent should follow in proportion to Gross Sales performance at any level.

If your Cost of Goods Sold expenses aren't proportionate in percent to your Gross Sales, either your budget is incorrect or you need to improve how you manage of these costs.

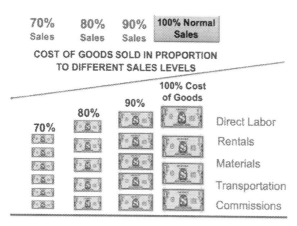

COST OF GOODS SOLD IN PROPORTION TO DIFFERENT SALES LEVELS

Emotion Over Logic

The Cost of Goods Sold expense category is typically managed reactively. Job costs in small companies are often created and paid for out of emotion over logic. The least restraint is placed on paying demanding suppliers, while the most lucrative customers are screaming at and badgering to deliver the products they've paid for.

Cost of Goods bills can be paid any time in the month. However, a policy for paying half the month's job costs by the middle of the month, and the other half at the end of the month helps to control cash flow and give you some time to think.

Paying less often, and more deliberately gives you that much needed extra time to think through and evaluate your decisions about your supply expenses and your supplier value. Did your suppliers deliver on their promises and give you what you bargained for?

Slowing down your supplier payments, tightening up your policies, and keeping to fewer pay days is highly recommended. This control is vital to better your overall cost planning.

"How much should my Cost of Goods Sold be?"

And now, a word on suppliers:

I believe that your strategic suppliers are those who have your best interest in mind. They are the ones who work at being good suppliers and who make a real effort to understand your vision and mission and your ups and downs. They are your long-term, most trusted partners who will gladly work with you on your payment terms.

The Goal: fewer, better suppliers get most of the work.

Safety first. Profit Second.

I've generally used a rule of thumb that the percentage of my Cost of Goods Sold to my Gross Sales is a factor of my overall business safety.

I am safer when my Cost of Goods Sold is less than 50% of my Gross Sales. I am not as concerned about a single vendor holding me up on their terms. I am less safe when my Cost of Goods Sold is more than 50% of my Gross Sales. If I am a distributor with Cost of Goods being 60%, I am 40% at risk. If my Cost of Goods is 70%, I am 30% safe. My Vendors could change policy on a dime, and I'd have to bow to their whims or give way to an uncontrollable industry movement.

If you are selling a high Cost of Goods Sold product or service, continue to look for other products in your mix to bring your Cost of Goods Sold into balance of 50% or less.

> **If you don't have a job, you don't have Cost of Goods Sold. Your balance of Cost of Goods Sold to Gross Sales is a safety factor. The lower the Cost of Goods percent of Gross Sales, the higher the percentage of business safety.**

True Story: The case for less, better supplier relationships

Tyler T, of Omaha, Nebraska had an electronics shop that sold cameras, lighting and security devices. Tyler never paid his suppliers on time or treated them properly. He would run up bills as far as they allowed him to and when they started to pressure him for payment, he would take his business to the next supplier.

This continued for quite a while. Tyler was severely in debt, and had taken advantage of all his key suppliers, but he didn't seem to care. His attitude was, "there's plenty more where that came from".

One day an industry manufacturer unexpectedly introduced a new technology for a unique self-charging battery, allowing its devices an additional two hours of emergency use before replacement. The key suppliers who Tyler mistreated were awarded exclusive distributorships. No one would sell to Tyler.

Needless to say, Tyler's business closed.

It's one thing to run into debt. It's harder to run into the suppliers. Key suppliers who are willing to understand and work with you are the lifeblood of a business. Those who value accountability and integrity, show respect through open, honest communication and seek collaborative problem-solving will build sustainable businesses.

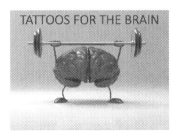

THREE COST OF GOODS SOLD TATTOOS FOR THE BRAIN

Here are three main takeaways for the Cost of Goods Sold of a Kanketa Balanced Budget.

#1. Nothing is a Cost of Goods Sold unless there is a customer that buys it and there is a verifiable job. No job? No Cost of Goods Sold.

#2. The lower the Cost of Goods percent to Gross Sales, the higher the percentage of business safety that exists.

#3 The goal of Cost of Goods Sold is to balance and market like-product types so that the percentage of Cost of Goods Sold to Net Sales is relatively constant from year to year.

MONEY OUT: THE MARGIN

Spend only what you can afford by keeping your Margin in balance.

Margin is Another Word for Gross Profit

If you were to ask 100 People how profitable their companies are, you are likely to get 100 different answers. For this reason, Kanketa avoids the confusion of the word "Gross Profit," and instead, calls it "Margin" (the difference between Net Sales and Cost of Goods Sold).

As you might have suspected by now, Kanketa has its own language. Earlier, in Chapter 2 we defined Normal as the ideal monthly sales performance level at which all resources are fully utilized without the need for further expense. Normal Monthly Margin will be used throughout this book. The Normal Monthly Margin is the money left after you remove Cost of Goods Sold and Cost of Quality at 100% "Normal" sales levels.

Margin is the only money that counts when you talk about company growth.

In Kanketa, your Normal Margin has six equally balanced parts:

1. FIXED PEOPLE COSTS (repeatable manager's salaries),
2. FIXED NON-PEOPLE COSTS (month-to-month, predictably repeatable overhead expenses necessary to maintain your business performance and profitability. All overhead costs that aren't manager salaries)
3. SEMI-VARIABLE PEOPLE COSTS (managers' pay that changes with performance)
4. SEMI-VARIABLE NON-PEOPLE COSTS (changing monthly overhead expenses necessary to grow your business and increase your profitability)
5. OWNER NET PROFIT FOR LATER
6. OWNER NET PROFIT FOR NOW

When all these budget components are equal, you have a Balanced Budget.

In other words, one-sixth of your monthly Margin at 100% Normal sales levels is your maximum monthly allowance for each of these expense categories.

The Kanketa goal is always balance. A company with a Balanced Budget is safe and healthy. With a Kanketa Balanced Budget, you can take the most money out of your business without damaging it while it continues to grow with or without your direct involvement.

Margin pays for all company overhead; the total costs required to operate the business every day, every month of every year, whether you have $1 of sales, or $1 million in sales. Operating costs pay for managers and Non-People Costs which are everything that is not a person, such as rent, utilities, phones, insurance, etc., as well as a Net Profit for the owner.

Some people incorrectly refer to Margin as "net income." More accurately, net income is the amount of money that is left after all the company's debts and expenses are subtracted from all its total income.

It's hardly a wonder why small business owners struggle with finance. There is a tremendous disconnect about the use of financial terms and their meanings.

WHAT IS BUSINESS GROWTH?

"Is my business growing, or just going."

Margin isn't everything. It's the only thing.

What would you say if someone told you that they can guarantee to double your revenue in two years? You'd probably feel pretty good, wouldn't you? Overjoyed would be a better word. After all, the company's profit has slipped a bit and doubling the revenue is going to really take care of things.

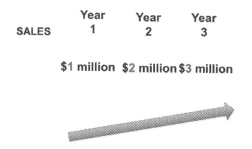

	Year 1	Year 2	Year 3
SALES			
	$1 million	$2 million	$3 million

Some companies believe that more sales will make up for shrinking Net Profit. This is unsustainable, and an extremely risky assumption that will more often than not bankrupt you.

	Yr. 1	Yr. 2	Yr. 3
SALES	$1 million	$2 million	$3 million
MARGIN	$ 500k	$ 400k	$ 300k
PROFIT	$ 165k	$ 130k	$ 100k

Here you will notice that doubled revenue has nothing to do with Net Profit. What is truly ironic is that all those large global companies that go bankrupt have high-paid, six-figure accounting wizards from the top business schools in the country on their payroll.

When a company makes a significant reinvestment to generate more sales in hopes of making up for shrinking Net Profit, it is taking its eyes off the ball.

So, why the bankruptcies when they can afford the best and most brilliant minds in the world? Perhaps, those six-figure accountants have the right ladder leaning against the wrong wall. They were using ticket sales to make decisions on the field, when all along they needed a playbook.

Declining sales makes most investors very nervous. Some companies had smart, experienced leadership who know the difference between variable, direct and indirect costs. They focused on Margins.

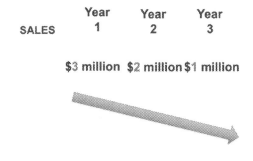

	Year 1	Year 2	Year 3
SALES	$3 million	$2 million	$1 million

2006: STARBUCKS

Take Starbucks for instance. Starbucks over-expanded, diluting profits and damaging the brand (not every corner needed a Starbucks).

2008 net income had fallen dramatically, cutting the stock price in half. Concentration on service, supply costs, pricing, operating efficiency and product expansion recovered the company.

In 2006, Starbucks made big leaps quickly and spent much of its profit trying to become the leader in the coffee market. Stock plummeted dramatically. After some surprising research, the Starbuck leaders found that they weren't really in the coffee business at all. They were in the neighborhood meeting place business, that just happened to sell good coffee.

Margin Increase

Starbucks repackaged itself as a meeting place with a whole new approach. The company was able to turn things around despite slipping sales. With a narrow concentration on service, the company restructured its supply costs and pricing, improved operational efficiency and incrementally and carefully expanded its product offerings.

	Yr. 1	Yr. 2	Yr. 3
SALES	$3 million	$2 million	$1 million
MARGIN	$ 300k	$ 400k	$ 500k
PROFIT	$ 100k	$ 130k	$ 165k

Starbucks wasn't the only one that responded wisely to its marketing problems.

McDonald's removed Ronald as its main character and began to concentrate on healthier food for the whole family. Coca-Cola competed against itself by buying up the competition. Apple computer reinvented its product line and diversified by adding Apple TV, steamy streaming video games, Apple iPad, Apple iPhone, Apple iTunes and many more. Marvel Comic Books marched head on into the movie business. Pabst Blue Ribbon went into the licensing business. Swatch attached the jewelry market and became more than a watch. Others followed. By focusing on Margin and the root causes of the low Margin problems, these companies alone rescued an estimated 3.2 million jobs.

Two Myths That Kill Small Companies

There are hundreds of stories that all lead to the same bad place because of two deadly business myths …

Myth #1: More revenue is meaningful growth.

Fact: More revenue does not reflect necessarily growth.

Myth #2: More loans and more funding will correct the problem.

Fact: Debt creates does not create growth.

There is nothing wrong with controlled business debt as long as the loaned amount

ultimately causes the debt to be eliminated.

A loan that does not produce at least three times return on investment can make a bigger problem than if you never invested the money at all.

Margin Growth is The Only Meaningful Growth.

The single most important idea that I want to convey in this section is that Margin growth is the only meaningful growth in your company.

Income minus debt equals Net Profit. Net Profit, properly reinvested, reduces debt and increases sales, which should grow Margin. Grow your Margin and you'll grow your company. Growing sales without growing Margin mathematically creates a predictable result: bankruptcy. This is how it all ties together.

> Margin isn't everything. It's the only thing. Margin, not Gross Sales, determines the real growth of the business.

MARGIN:
FIXED COSTS AND SEMI-VARIABLE COSTS

In The Margin Two Types of Costs Must Be In Balance.

These are costs that operate the business day in and day out – Fixed Costs and Semi-Variable Costs. I will dedicate a chapter to each type of cost. For now, I will clarify the difference between them.

Margin Has Fixed Costs

Fixed Costs are repeatable costs that DO NOT change significantly from month to month – such as rent, insurance, cell phone contracts, etc. This includes Fixed employee salaries.

Margin Has Semi-Variable Costs

Semi-Variable are costs that DO change from month to month, such as car repairs, office supplies, gas, etc. Semi-Variable Costs also include employee performance bonuses.

Net Profit is in the Margin but is a completely separate topic, not part of this discussion.

Your goal is to use the monthly averages of the previous year's income and expenses, to achieve an equal balance between:

People and Non-People Costs
and Fixed and Semi-Variable Costs
at Normal (100% ideal performance) sales levels

When you achieve this, the Net Profit will follow.

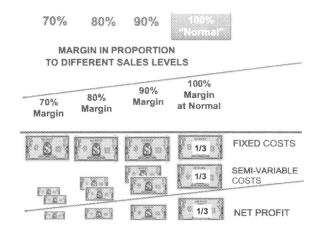

Financial balance is the point at which Fixed
Costs and Semi-Variable Costs are equal.
Financial balance only occurs at 100% Normal,
creating the most safety for the business.

TWO TYPES OF MARGIN:
EQUALIZED VS. BALANCED

Kanketa teaches "Safety First. Profit Second." You can make all the profit possible, but still lose your company in bankruptcy (Toys R Us, K-Mart, US Airways, Radio Shack - the list goes on). In some of these companies, the Fixed Costs were too high. In others, there wasn't sufficient Net Profit available in time to pay for the escalating out of control debts.

The Kanketa Balanced Margin keeps debt under control with always enough profit in the Margin to pay for it, but...

Margin isn't Margin isn't Margin. In Kanketa, there is an "Equalized Margin" and a "Balanced Margin." Both create the same profitability with the exception that a Balanced Margin is safer than an Equalized Margin.

An equalized company is a profitable company, but it is not necessarily safe from unexpected changes that happen suddenly in the marketplace.

A balanced company is both a safe, and profitable company. A Balanced Margin is the company's first line of defense and will contain the safe profit and expense levels.

EQUALIZED MARGIN

An Equalized Margin exists when either Fixed overhead costs or the Semi-Variable overhead costs exceed the other, but the Net Profit still remains at one-third of the Margin at Normal.

In both cases shown, the net-profit is one-third of the total Margin.

Example A:

Total monthly Margin is $12,000,
Monthly Fixed Costs are $5,000,
Semi-Variable Costs are $3,000,
and the net-profit of one-third of the Margin is $ 4,000.

The Margin is equalized.

Example B:

Total monthly Margin is $12,000,
Monthly Fixed Costs are $2,500,
Semi-Variable Costs are $5,500,
and the Net Profit is one-third of the Margin: $4,000.

The Margin is equalized

A Balanced Budget at Normal sales levels exists when the budget of Fixed Costs and Semi-Variable Costs in the Margin equal each other. When this happens, Net Profit is automatically an equal one-third.

The budget for each of the three components is exactly one-third of the total Margin at Normal.

BALANCED MARGIN

3 EQUAL PARTS

1/3 FIXED COSTS

1/3 SEMI-VARIABLE COSTS

1/3 NET PROFIT

Example C:

Total monthly Margin is $12,000,
Monthly Fixed cost budget is $4,000,
Monthly Semi-Variable cost budget is $4,000,
Net Profit budget is one-third of the Margin - $4,000.

The Margin is balanced.

> **A company with an equalized Margin
> is a profitable, but not a safe company.
> A balanced company is both safe and profitable.**

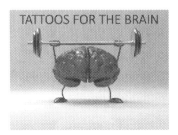

THREE MARGIN TATTOOS FOR THE BRAIN

Here are three main takeaways for the Margin of a Kanketa Balanced Budget

#1. Margin percent of Net Sales parallels sales performance.

#2. Margin is the only factor that determines the growth of a business.

#3. The Kanketa balanced Margin keeps debt under control with always enough profit in the Margin to pay for it.

True Story: Net Profit in an Unsafe but Equalized Budget

For 14 years Troy and Danielle ran a successful recruiting company of 27 employees in Dublin, Ohio.

The company consistently made a Net Profit every month between $8,000 and $10,000 after all expenses. Then, unexpectedly the business changed drastically for the worst when many industries sought lower labor costs in other countries. The couple had to reduce their labor force by half within 60 days to maintain the same Net Profit that they had counted on for years. Within a month after the reduction in workforce, their profit diminished to half. Following more cuts to survive, Troy and Danielle were now down to eight employees. Needless to say, the Net Profit continued to dwindle until their company went bankrupt and their building was sold at an auction.

The Net Profit remained at a consistent percent of the Margin throughout.

The percentage of Fixed Costs and Semi-Variable Costs expanded and contracted.
The company was equalized and the Net Profit was the highest that the Margin allowed, but the budget was not balanced. Consequently, the company was not safe.

CHAPTER 5:

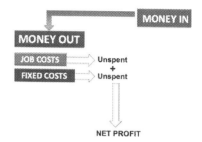

FIXED COSTS

"How much should my business expenses be every month?"
"How much should I pay my People?"

Fixed Costs Give the Company Stability

Fixed Costs are the predictable, repeatable costs to create and maintain company stability by keeping the doors open.

PEOPLE COSTS ARE YOUR MANAGERS. NON-PEOPLE COSTS ARE YOUR OVERHEAD OPERATING COSTS. BOTH ARE FIXED, AND SEMI-VARIABLE.

The goal is to keep Fixed People and fixed Non-People Costs equal to, and in balance with each other.

Keep Fixed People and Fixed Non-People Costs equal to, and in balance with each other.

Fixed expenses are recurring costs in repeatable amounts that do not change from month to month.

Fixed Costs break down further into:

Fixed People Costs

and Fixed Non-People Costs.

> **People Costs in the Margin are your managers. Non-People Costs are your operating overhead expenses.**

From month to month, your business has certain costs that do not significantly change. You have Fixed Costs whether you have $1 of business, or $1 million dollars of business.

FIXED PEOPLE COSTS
Fixed People Costs are the repeatable salaries of your managers who must show up for work, whether you sell $1 or $1 million. Their work is spread over all jobs.

FIXED NON-PEOPLE COSTS
Non-People Costs are all recurring overhead operating expenses of the business that are not People. Rent is a Fixed Cost that does not change. An Insurance payment is a Fixed Cost that does not change. Cellphone contracts are Fixed Costs that do not change. Leases are Fixed Costs that do not change. Whether sales are way up, or way down, these are Fixed Costs that are constant and unchanging from month to month.

Eight Main Fixed Cost Categories:

1. Manager Salaries
2. Advertising
3. Insurances (other than health)
4. Interest
5. Monthly Service Contracts
6. Equipment and Vehicle Leases
7. Office Lease or Rent
8. Miscellaneous – All Other

Fixed COSTS **DO NOT** change
with sales performance

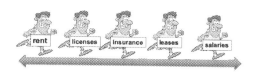

Sub-categories of Expenses

Within each of these main cost categories are subcategories of expense items. For example, in the category of people you will have different managers. One will oversee products and production. One will charge ahead in the marketing arena. There might be an HR manager or a customer service manager.

In the Non-People expense categories such as equipment leases, there are Fixed Costs that include recurring cell phone contracts and car leases. In the office expense category, you will find Fixed contracts for outside services such as cleaning and maintenance contracts, accounting and professional service contracts, and so on.

Don't list the main Kanketa expense categories on your P&L. If you are going to list anything alphabetically, then alphabetize the sub-categories.

Examples of RECURRING MONTHLY CONTRACTS

- Cleaning - Janitorial Services
- Dues and Subscriptions
- Internet Service
- Phone - Landline
- Phone - cell
- Security
- Software Licenses – Contracts
- Technology Service Contracts
- Waste Removal

> **Fixed Costs do not change monthly by more than 5%.**
> **Semi-Variable Costs do change monthly in 10% performance increments.**

IS MY BUSINESS SET UP TO MAKE A PROFIT?

There are millions of businesses that make a healthy profit without the Kanketa method. You don't need Kanketa to be successful. That said, I'd like to take a page or two to explain the question: Is my business set up to make a profit? Am I in complete control of the profit that I expect or does Net Profit just show up?

Many small businesses pay salaries according to market demand; not what they can afford. This is typically because many businesses are not structured to make money. Redundancy and inefficiency are built into their system.

In the 1940s, following World War II, when millions of Americans returned to work, there were severe job shortages. The U.S. way of life redesigned itself. Family-run businesses were organized and grew from loving parents who, wanting to provide for their children, built companies with the sole purpose of creating secure jobs, but not necessarily with the vision of creating significant financial futures. Out of this survival motivation grew our American college-taught organizational chart which is used today. I prefer to call this the "Importance Chart."

If you inherited a business and nearly all of your business knowledge came from hard- working parents; or you started a business and learned it by osmosis; or you went to a business college and learned it in a business theory class; or perhaps you had a mentor who had a successful business career back when, you have probably been taught the Importance Chart along the way.

The Importance Chart is a traditional hierarchical business model borrowed from large companies by small companies, purely from the lack of any other useful models. In my opinion it does not work, nor does it have a place in today's small business world. By its very design, it promotes separation between people who should be in constant collaboration. It is a model of who's more important, who's making more money and who can't talk to whom.

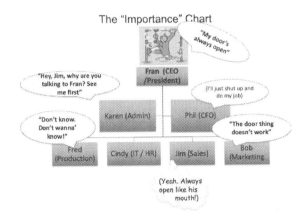

The "Importance" Chart

Ever since I can remember, this business model has always bothered me. In the 1960s, the guy at the end of the hall with the big window was the important guy. He had the most pictures on his wall, and a new grey carpet.

Back then, your importance was visible to the company based on the location of your office, the size and type of pictures on your wall, and the color of the furniture in your room. Grey carpet and couches and leather chairs with brass studded arm rests were most important, followed by navy and Naugahyde. Meaningless titles were on every business card. Few people in the company had true empowerment.

Clearly, the leadership methods were very different back then. If you ever have a chance to watch Madmen, you'll know what I mean. The series premiered on July 19, 2007 on cable network AMC. It is available in many places. It was extremely well produced. The producers didn't miss a detail. If you want to understand how companies were managed in the 1960s, watch this series.

Business was operated and managed under the importance system. It was nothing but a political fishbowl. Prevailing attitudes of employees were "I don't dare to contribute. I don't care to contribute. I'd better just shut my mouth, do my job and collect my paycheck. I don't want to get fired for my opinions". Ironically, the big guy at the end of the hall would periodically stick his head out of the door and yell, "My door is always open." All the while, the employees were saying to themselves under their breath …
"yeah, and you need to get that door hinge fixed".

Mike Wolf

FLAT ORGANIZATIONS
not

<u>FLAT JOB DESCRIPTIONS!</u>

No Empowerment. Political.   Just do your job.

Kanketa promotes a "flat organization" as a specific way to look at and how to operate your business so that it always maintains a healthy balance of accountability and empowerment between everyone who works in it. In Kanketa every employee contributes and is compensated on equal terms.

So, why should you bother with this if it's going to create more work for you?

Do you really want more accountability? Are you looking to wrap yourself around the discomfort of change? Why not just run the business the way you've always done it and continue to make money? In fact, why have employees at all? Just make it YOU and avoid the hassle.

Many solopreneuers brag about how much money they make without having to deal with the headaches of employees. Please hear me out. There is significant long-term value in going through the difficult process of building a staff of loyal, key employees.

True Story: Build Workrooms, Not Walls

Steve W. of Bloomington, Illinois. had three full time managers plus himself in his retail shop. The managers were required to show up whether there was $1 or $1 million dollars of business.

When Steve bought the company three years before, he inherited the problems of existing positions. One of the managers was his brother-in-law. The other two were in the family of the friend from whom he bought the company.

There were no clear positions or job descriptions. Since nothing was written, every day was a fight over who was doing what, when and why. Misunderstandings ran high over who was contributing more. Much time was wasted daily over arguments of the smallest responsibilities. Production errors escalated by default. Eventually, the managers quit and started their own competitive companies. Over the next ten years, the owners of each of their own companies made the equivalent of what they would have made as a salary working for Steve, without a decade of hassle and ill-feelings.

The difference between a high-performing, high-profit company and any company that is not growing, just going, is clarity of responsibilities set in place in writing on day one. In a balanced company, no management position is worth more or less than the other. Every manager receives the same Fixed base salary. Each is individually empowered to earn more based on company performance.

THE KANKETA HOUSE OF VALUE

The KANKETA ideogram tells many stories.

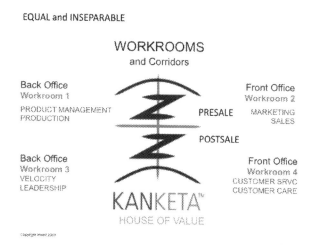

EQUAL and INSEPARABLE

WORKROOMS
and Corridors

Back Office
Workroom 1

PRODUCT MANAGEMENT
PRODUCTION

PRESALE

POSTSALE

Front Office
Workroom 2

MARKETING
SALES

Back Office
Workroom 3
VELOCITY
LEADERSHIP

Front Office
Workroom 4
CUSTOMER SRVC
CUSTOMER CARE

KANKETA™
HOUSE OF VALUE

This ideogram is a business plan, a financial plan, an organizational plan, a physical store, a physical office and a plant layout, a leadership model and many other constructs. For our purposes, we will see this symbol as a business structure and a design for a "House of Value," with virtual rooms and walls, doors and corridors.

The Kanketa House of Value is divided into four equal and inseparable parcels - "Workrooms", with connecting rooms of equal size. The Workrooms each have one of the four functional purposes: make something, sell something, deliver something and service the people in need.

WORKROOMS AND CORRIDORS

"How many managers do I need?"

THE ANSWER: Enough managers to efficiently carry out the eight fundamental functions of every business on the globe, for starters. Four managers will be needed in a company of 30 employees or less, one for each Workroom.

Over the years I have observed successful Kanketa-based small companies with no more than four managers, efficiently, effectively and consistently producing up to $5 million a year in Gross Sales.

Each of the Workrooms is divided into "corridors". Each Workroom carries two related job descriptions for managing and delivering results, one measurable result for each corridor. Each Kanketa manager is responsible for the two corridors in their Workroom.

The lower corridor in each Workroom relies on its upper big sister corridor to produce, before its functions can be can fully and effectively carried out. In Kanketa...

- A business will need marketing before sales
- product management before production
- velocity (delivery) before self-directed leadership
- customer service before customer care

Top corridor first. Bottom corridor second.

A Business Leader is needed at the center of the business to keep all the corridors in motion, to carry out the vision and mission of the owner, and to report to the owner.

The back office on left side of the House is comprised of the MAKE and DELIVER Workrooms. In the front office, there are the SELL and SERVICE

Workrooms. The front office deals with the marketplace and shakes hands with the external customers. The back office people serve and treat the front office people as their internal customers.

House Rules

Any manager may participate in any Workroom where they are needed, when they are needed. However, there is always one Workroom manager who is the ultimate authority with the overriding responsibility for his/her Workroom. Each Workroom is equal to and inseparable from the others. In the Kanketa House of Value, no Workroom is of greater or lesser importance, nor are the people in it.

KANKETA HOUSE OF VALUE

Internal Customers → **KANKETA HOUSE of VALUE** External Customers →	
PRODUCT Mgt. Matl's Mgt / Costing Supply Chain Management	**MARKETING** Marketing Research / Pricing Lead Generation
PRODUCTION Total Quality / Error Free Ready-For-Use	PRE-SALE **SALES** Close 1st X Business Contract Management
VELOCITY Total Waste Reduction Productivity, Efficiency	BUSINESS LEADER **CUSTOMER SERVICE** Order Management POST-SALE Order Processing
LEADERSHIP Employee Active Listening Employee Engagement	**CUSTOMER CARE** Retention / Recovery Customers for Life

2.03-1 copyright mwolf 2012

INDIRECT EMPLOYEES

An indirect employee is not paid to do a specific job. Indirect employees must show up for work whether there is one job, or a hundred jobs, whether you sell $1 or $1 million dollars. An Indirect employee may be full time or part time.

Your managers are your "indirect" employees. They must show up whether you have $1 or $1 million dollars of work. Their work is spread out over the entire company. They do parts of all the jobs needed to run the company. They are hired to do whatever is needed, and whatever it takes.

Headcount

There is a practice among large companies to balance their budgets by managing and measuring overall productivity and to control profit by headcount. Headcount says that the total sales of the company divided by the number of people in the company equals the average dollar amount that each person is contributing. This number is again measured against national averages across each industry to determine the number of people that the company should keep employed. Companies hire and fire on this basis.

This practice allows some accountant to make financial decisions without considering who is being hired and fired and why. Jack Welch of GE automatically fired the 10 percent lowest performers without looking sideways, no questions asked.

My perspective only: Considering that it costs five times or more to hire and train a new employee than it does to retrain and re-motivate an existing one, companies of 30 or less should focus on retraining, reassigning and repurposing if possible. Let the large companies crumble under their own weight as their accountants continue to play out by their inefficient, worn and dated, valueless rules. Balancing a company by headcount might make sense to some bean counter, but to me, it makes no sense and has no place in the Kanketa House of Value for today's high performing small business.

Repositioning Talent

Perhaps an underperforming employee in one area can be trained to cultivate and support a new industry that the company doesn't currently have or support an existing industry with processes to bring in another $100,000.

The owner of a Kanketa business will do everything possible to take this second path, rather than firing a person because of a headcount-to-profit ratio.

PEOPLE COSTS: MANAGER SALARY

"Am I paying my people too much?" Not enough?

Pay Managers One-Half of Their Compensation to Maintain the Business

In Kanketa, one-half of a Workroom manager's job ... or 10 hours a week per corridor is budgeted to ensure that the corridor and the company doesn't slide backward and lose money. This protection takes a specific list of manager tasks that must be carried out.

... and One Half to Grow the Business

The other half of a Workroom manager's job, or 10 hours a week for each corridor should be dedicated to grow the company and increase Margin and profit. This is a specific list of manager tasks that are carried out.

In the growth area, the activities in each corridor are equally subdivided into two parts: The manager is rewarded for five hours a week of individual contribution to growth, and five hours a week for his/her team's contribution growth.

This is proven to be an effective structure, since a poorly-performing team may not hold back a high-performing individual, and a low-performing individual may not put drag on a high-performing team.

Corridor Teams

The corridor teams are uniquely defined by the business owner. Some companies design their teams horizontally, with a team member from an upper Workroom paired with a team from a lower Workroom (example: Product Manager from the MAKE Workroom and the Velocity Manager from the DELIVER Workroom. Others choose to reward front office and back office managers for individuals as well as team performance. While Team definitions differ from business to business, there are specific job functions that compliment each other.

In a team, Marketing compliments sales. Marketing in the upper SELL Workroom can also work well with Customer Service. Sales in the upper SELL Workroom (Pre-sale) can also work well with Customer Care (Post Sale). In a team, product management compliments production. Product Management in the upper MAKE Workroom (Pre-Sale) can also work well with Velocity (DELIVERY) in the lower Workroom (Post-Sale).

Manager Pay Scales

Standing back, this model creates one big question about employee compensation. If the Workrooms and corridors are equal and inseparable, if no one is more or less important than the other, if every corridor is ultimately responsible to deliver a single result, if everyone is accountable and empowered and if the company is truly a balanced, flat organization – then what about salaries? Is anyone paid more or less than the others?

Each of the four Workroom managers in the Kanketa House of Value is initially responsible for carrying out two job descriptions. One-half of a Workroom manager's job or 10 hours a week is the maximum time budgeted to maintain the performance of one corridor in a Workroom. Maintaining the performance of two corridors should take one manager less than 20 hours a week.

Once a company hovers around 30 employees, the corridor responsibilities begin to expand and require their own full-time corridor managers.

Begin by Paying Managers for Two Workrooms

Kanketa expects at least 75% of every week to be total billable results from each manager. In other words, a Workroom manager will spend four hours a week, managing a corridor in meetings, and in non-value-added time, with 16 hours of on-the-job billable time to its internal and external customers.

"I am both an owner and a manager in my business. How much should I pay myself?"

This depends upon what corridors you cover, and why and how you pay yourself.

The answer is: pay yourself a salary separately as a Workroom manager. Pay yourself from the Net Profit as the owner. More to come on this.

Corridors of Responsibility

What corridors in your House of Value are you personally covering every day everyone when you work in your business? What are you most passionate about when you work in your business?

Are you most passionate about …

Product Management? Researching and creating new products? Finding and managing suppliers?

Production? Doing the work hands on? Ensuring that each product is error free?

Velocity? Scheduling and delivery of products and services?

Human Resources? Ensuring that employees are happy and productive?

Marketing? Finding and creating new opportunities from new, first time prospects?

Sales? Proposing and closing jobs and converting prospects into paying contracts?

Customer Service? Making sure that each new customer is satisfied with every transaction during their experience?

Customer Care? Creating reasons to have customers keep coming back?

Don't pay more to yourself for any of these positions than you pay to other managers..

You'll create imbalance. When you eventually decide to replace yourself, you will be paying your salary as a Workroom manager to your replacement.

I will cover this topic later in the Net Profit chapter.

> **Workroom managers have two responsibilities.**
> **The upper corridor must be in place first.**
> **The lower corridor follows.**

FIXED PEOPLE COSTS ARE ONLY
FOUND IN THE MARGIN
(50% To Maintain Company Performance)

Manager Salaries

Once again, Fixed People Costs are the (pre-tax) gross salaries that must be paid to any indirect employees whether you have $1 of business, or $1 million dollars of business. The People Costs in your Margin pay your managers.

Now, you are probably asking yourself, "Aren't my managers' salaries a Fixed Cost? They are paid the same salary from month to month."

The answer is yes, and maybe.

Yes, your Fixed People Costs are the salaries in the Margin that do not change from month to month. However, not everything that is paid to your managers is a Fixed salary.

Kanketa does not support, promote or encourage totally Fixed salaries. Instead, Kanketa divides a manager's compensation equally into 50% Fixed salary and 50% for Performance Compensation.

In Kanketa, the Fixed manager salaries are paid to maintain company performance and to avoid the Gross Sales, Margin and Net Profit of the company from slipping.

Fixed People Costs are in place to ensure that the company doesn't lose money while it continues to grow. In Kanketa, there is a specific list of maintenance work – everything it takes to prevent each position, each Workroom and the total company performance from declining in profitability.

Fixed salaries pay for loss prevention activities.

Pay managers 50% of their total compensation for maintaining their Workroom performance, and additional compensation for increasing their Workroom performance and profitability.

When Fixed Costs Change Slightly

Fixed salaries are operational costs that do not change from month to month and fit with the other Fixed Costs of the company: rent, insurance payments, recurring contracts such as cellphones, car payments, and so on.

Some salaries might not remain exactly the same to the penny for the year. You might have a good reason to increase a person's Fixed salary during the year.

For the sake of practicality, let's say that all Fixed Costs generally do not change by more than 5% in any month from the previous month.

> **Fixed Costs generally do not change from month to month by more than 5%.**

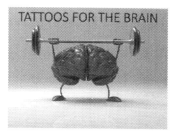

THREE FIXED COST TATTOOS FOR THE BRAIN

Here are three main takeaways for the Fixed Costs of a Kanketa Balanced Budget.

#1. Fixed Costs are 33% of monthly Margin at 100% Normal, 16.65% salaries and 16.65% Non-People overhead costs.

#2. Fixed Costs do not change by more than 5% from month to month

#3. In Kanketa, all Fixed Costs for the month are paid by the 10th

True Story: Out of Balance Fixed Costs Can Really Fix You... For Good!

Jason L, of Lansing, Michigan inherited his father's bicycle shop of 18 years. In his effort to create an efficient hands off business, Jason negotiated as many costs as possible to be Fixed. Jason believed that if all of his costs were the same from month to month, his bookkeeping would be a breeze and he'd have less accounting work to do. The salaries of his 5 employees were the same every month. His operating costs were the same. He held to a strict auto allowance that didn't change, a rigid office expense budget with a Fixed budget for trash pickup, office supplies and a Fixed monthly retainer for his accountant.

Every annual bill was divided by 12 and he sent the payments monthly. This was fine at first. Sales were stable and steady from month to month and Jas made a nice profit. Later as the months went by, the bicycle industry started to change. The market's appetite for the younger bikes in Jason's inventory went to lighter weight exercise bikes for older People. Added to this the increased price of steel increased the cost of new inventories with a whole new line of tools to repair them. Sales gradually declined to an average of 60% of Normal levels and Jason had to lay off his technicians. Since everyone was so acclimated to a steady paycheck, there was no flexibility to negotiate wages. In the following year Jason was down to 2 technicians and had to move to a small location half the size. The Net Profit declined

---

Jason's company was too anchored with Fixed Costs. By not balancing his business, he was unable to move with the changing market. This inflexibility is the same problem that unions create.

NOTE: All case studies used in this book are based on actual situations. The names and business types in the examples have been slightly altered to protect the business owners.

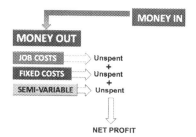

CHAPTER 6

SEMI-VARIABLE COSTS

All along I have been talking about costs that do not change significantly from month to month. Yet, from month to month, your business also has overhead costs that DO change.

Semi-Variable Costs are company expense types that you will always have, but they will change slightly every month, up and down, with the sales performance of the business.

When sales are higher than 100% Normal, you will put more gas in your car to service customers. When your sales are lower than 100% Normal, you will use less gas to service customers. When your sales are higher than 100% Normal, you will use more postage, more office supplies, more electricity. When your sales are lower than 100% Normal, you will use less postage, fewer office supplies, and less electricity.

You will always have these types of Semi-Variable operating costs, but they will move up and down slightly as the sales of your company increases and decreases. These costs are called Semi-Variable because they are always there, but they breathe with the performance of the company.

Twelve Main Semi-Variable Cost Categories:

1. Manager Performance Pay
2. Employee Benefits
3. Office Supplies
4. Professional Fees
5. General Repairs and Maintenance (not vehicles)
6. Licenses and Permits
7. Taxes
8. Vehicle Repairs and Maintenance
9. Travel (cost of vehicle operation: fuel, oil, parking etc.)
10. Customer Meals and Entertainment
11. Utilities
12. Miscellaneous – all other

The Goal of a Balanced Budget.

The goal is to make Fixed People Costs equal to Semi-Variable People Costs and Fixed Non-People Costs equal to Semi-Variable Non-People Costs at 100% Normal performance.

Budget 10 hours a week per manager to maintain each corridor and 10 hours a week per manager to grow each corridor. Expect 75% total billable time each week from every manager.

> **Fixed Costs pay for maintaining
> company stability.
> Semi-Variable Costs pay for creating growth.**

MANAGER PERFORMANCE COMPENSATION
(For Creating Company Growth)

"Am I paying (my people) too much? Not enough?"
"How much should I pay my people?"
"When can I give a raise and how much?"

Semi-Variable People Costs: Performance Compensation for Company Growth

The question isn't "How much should I pay my people?" A better question to ask is "How much am I willing to pay my people for helping to grow the company?"

Growth is accomplished by ensuring that the company has increased opportunities to win by increasing revenue and Margin and reducing costs. Kanketa encourages that employee salaries are balanced, with one-half paid for maintenance to keep the company in place and stable, and one-half performance to keep the company in a growth mode. By balancing a manager's maintenance responsibilities with a list of growth activities, including everything it takes to grow the profitability of the employee's position and the Workroom, you will create an overall consistent company performance.

Need some ideas? Call me.

Individual and Team Performance Pay

Some global companies balance Workrooms further by balancing compensation between Semi-Variable team contributions and Semi-Variable Individual performance. In this way, if the team isn't performing, the individual isn't held back from overachieving. Conversely, if the individual is underperforming, the team isn't penalized.

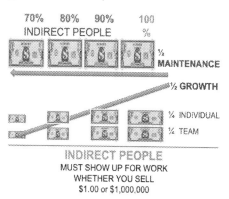

70% 80% 90% 100%
INDIRECT PEOPLE %
½ MAINTENANCE
½ GROWTH
¼ INDIVIDUAL
¼ TEAM

INDIRECT PEOPLE
MUST SHOW UP FOR WORK
WHETHER YOU SELL
$1.00 or $1,000,000

"When can I give my employees a raise? How Much?"

Give raises once a year to everyone on the management team based on the prior year's performance. In Kanketa, everyone gets a raise at the same time with the new budget because raises are based on Margins, not emotions.

In the previous chapter on Fixed Costs, I established that 50% of your People compensation at Normal should be Fixed. In Kanketa, any more than this throws the compensation budget out of balance and the company's safety out the window. The company is overpaying for less value than it is receiving.

Kanketa teaches that managers should have performance bonuses when they do a good job. Consequently, their bonus compensation would logically be different from month to month. Semi-Variable "People" compensation is the (pre-tax) gross pay to your managers for their ability to grow the company. Semi-Variable pay is performance pay.

In Kanketa, the purpose of Semi-Variable compensation to managers is to reward them for increased company performance.

How much of a raise?

Before you give a raise, be sure your fix salary levels are at 8.33% of Margin at Normal (.0833) for every active manager that you have hired for a Workroom - from 1 to 4 managers (including you as the owner). The goal is to cover all Workrooms first.

After you have achieved this, put Semi-Variable Performance Compensation in place. Your managers are now being paid equally to maintain, and paid individually for performance to grow their Workrooms. At a glance...

Margin at 100% Normal X 4.17% is the monthly Fixed salary paid to each manager's to maintain his/her Workroom. Fixed salaries are paid by the 10th of the month.

Performance Margin X 4.17% is the manager's monthly Semi-Variable performance compensation to grow their Workroom. Semi-Variable performance is paid on or before the 25th.

MANAGER PERFORMANCE PAY SCHEDULE

PERFORMANCE COMPENSATION – 4.17% OF PERFORMANCE MARGIN

Once a month, by the 25th, each manager should receive the second half of his/her pay for improving the profitability of their department. Performance Compensation is based on the company's previous month's performance Margin.

1. The previous month's Margin is **100%** of Margin at 100% Normal.
   Example: At a Margin of **$95,000** at Normal, the manager's performance compensation by the 25th of the following month will be $95,000 X **100%** Normal Margin X .0417 (in this case: **$3,962**).

2. The previous month's Margin is **90%-99%** of the above 100% Normal Margin.
   Example: At a Margin that falls between $85,500 and $94,999, the manager's performance compensation on the 25th of the following month will be $95,000 X **90%** of Normal Margin X .0417 (in this case: **$3,387**).

3. The previous month's Margin is **80%-89%** of the above 100% Normal Margin.
   Example: At a Margin that falls between $76,000 and $85,499, the manager's performance compensation by the 25th of the following month will be $95,000 X **80%** of Normal Margin X .0417 (in this case: **$3,011**).

4. The previous month's Margin is **70%-79%** of the above 100% Normal Margin.
   Example: At a Margin that falls between $66,500 and $75,999, the manager's performance compensation on the 25th of the following month will be $95,000 X **70%** of Normal Margin X .0417 (in this case: **$2,773**).

5. The previous month's Margin is **60%-69%** of the above 100% Normal Margin.
   Example: At a Margin that falls between $57,000 and $66,499, the manager's performance compensation on the 25th of the following month will be $95,000 X **60%** of Normal Margin X .0417 (in this case: **$2,377**).

6. The previous month's Margin is **50%-59%** of the above 100% Normal Margin.
   Example: At a Margin that falls between $47,500 - $56,999, the manager's performance compensation on the 25th of the following month will be $95,000 X **50%** of Normal Margin X .0417 (in this case: **$1,980**).

SEMI-VARIABLE NON-PEOPLE OVERHEAD
(TO SUPPORT COMPANY GROWTH)

In Kanketa, the Semi-Variable Non-People expenses are routine, familiar onthly repeating operational costs, but not as predictable or repeatable as Fixed Costs. These costs change slightly up or down with sales performance.

Semi-Variable Non-People Costs in the Margin are all overhead costs that support growth as the sales performance of the business increases. Semi-Variable Non-People Costs can produce and control cost savings.

UTILITIES?

OFFICE SUPPLIES?

AUTO MAINTENANCE?

POSTAGE?   ETC.

Semi-variable COSTS DO change slightly with sales performance

Transparency with Employees

The budgets are equal in all Workrooms.

I believe in transparency with employees whenever possible. Employees talk and eventually they will all hear the story. You might as might as well accurately present your side up front so that they all hear it in the way that you intend it to be heard.

If you are an employer who chooses to be private with your employees when discussing compensation, this will give you a tool for giving individual raises privately as you see progress and effort. Because your Cost of Goods performance follows your sales performance percent of Normal proportionately, your Margin should also reflect the sales performance percentage. If it doesn't, your Cost of Goods Sold might not be well managed. Keep in mind that while your Margin is in proportion to sales, your Fixed Non-People Costs in your Margin always remain consistent, while your Semi-Variable Non-People Costs are changing.

The Significant Benefit of Semi-Variable Cost Management:

The benefit of balancing Fixed Costs with Semi-Variable Costs is financial safety for all.

Job Safety

Many large global companies begin layoffs at approximately 70% of Normal sales performance. The Kanketa budget is designed so that at any performance level above 50% of Normal, all costs including manager compensation are always paid. In other words, at 50% of Normal performance, a manager will still have a job if the company's sales suddenly and unexpectedly drop in half.

Example: Most Kanketa-based Japanese companies like Toyota, Suzuki, Kawasaki, etc. kept all of their employees in place following the tsunami which devastated Japan in 2011.

Company safety

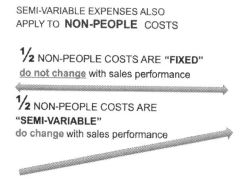

SEMI-VARIABLE EXPENSES ALSO APPLY TO **NON-PEOPLE** COSTS

$\frac{1}{2}$ NON-PEOPLE COSTS ARE **"FIXED"**
do not change with sales performance

$\frac{1}{2}$ NON-PEOPLE COSTS ARE **"SEMI-VARIABLE"**
do change with sales performance

Semi-Variable Costs apply to Non-People expenses as well. The only time that Fixed Costs and Semi-Variable Costs are equal to each other is in the budget at 100% Normal. All the rest of the time, while Fixed People and Fixed Non-People Costs do not change, the Semi-Variable People and Non-People Costs are budgeted to change at each sales performance level.

How much change? The little ten percent makes 100% of the difference.

Kanketa measures performance in 10% change increments. In Kanketa, the Semi-Variable People and Non-People Costs change monthly at each sales performance level by 10%,. The Semi-Variable amounts increase and decrease slightly from one month to the next by 10% as sales rise and fall.

When the overall sales revenue increases or decreases in one month, the managers are paid from the performance column accordingly in the following month.

How Semi-Variable Expenses Work

THE KANKETA GOLDEN RULE:

Last month's performance (total <u>sales)</u> determines this month's budget.
(See my book: "The Kanketa 30-day Money Map")

If the business performs at 70% of Normal in a month, then Kanketa can only afford to pay those responsible 70% of Normal for that month in the following month.

If the overall business increases in a month by 10% <u>above</u> Normal performance, then Kanketa rewards those responsible with a Performance Compensation increase of 110% of Normal for that month in the following month.

Semi-Variable expenses also apply to Non-People overhead in the same manner.

Semi-Variable Non-People Expenses:

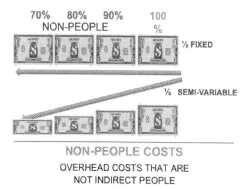

NON-PEOPLE COSTS
OVERHEAD COSTS THAT ARE
NOT INDIRECT PEOPLE

If the overall business performs at 60% of Normal in a month, then Kanketa only allows 60% of the Normal budget for its overhead for the following month.

In this case the budget in the following month would be 60% for gas for the car, 60% for office supplies, 60% for utilities, etc.

If the overall business decreases from Normal in a month by 30%, which is 70% of the Normal budget, a 30% budget decrease follows in utilities, gas for the car, office supplies, etc., paid in the following month.

When you are trying to maintain a balanced company, it's the little 10% that makes 100% of the difference.

> **The monthly budget follows sales performance and increases or decreases from the 100% Normal performance column in 10% increments.**

OVERSPENT AND UNSPENT: WHEN COSTS DON'T FIT THE BUDGET

Overspent
When the actual Fixed Costs or Semi-Variable Costs exceed their budget, the budget will show a negative overage as a line item. If any budget is overspent, the company is not balanced.

Unspent
When either Fixed or Semi-Variable budgets have money left over after all expenses are paid, the budgets are underspent. The unspent money is available at any moment for unexpected changes that might occur within the current year. It will be rare that Fixed Costs exactly equal Semi-Variable Costs. One will almost always exceed the other. This is handled by simply adding an additional "unspent" line to each budget.

Update the Budget One Time Per Year
Fixed and Semi-Variable Costs can be different each year. Kanketa recommends only revising the budget once a year at the beginning of the new calendar or fiscal year of business. When you separate all your monthly Non-People Costs into Fixed and Semi-Variable expense categories, you might find more costs on one side or the other. You should do everything possible to balance them out. This typically does not happen immediately, but there are many ways to get this to happen over time.

Some expenses might be Fixed Costs one year such as a monthly legal or accounting retainer that can be moved to a Semi-Variable payment as needed the next year. At 100% Normal sales levels the business is in balance when Indirect People Fixed Costs equal People Semi-Variable, and Non-People Fixed Costs equal Non-People Semi-Variable Costs. Both Fixed and Semi-Variable budgets have a category in place for unspent money. Any unspent money that is not used for unexpected changes that might occur within the current year becomes a contribution to Net Profit at midnight of the last day of the month.

True Story: Semi-Variable Honesty Always Wins

Colin's Engineering firm of 17 employees was the bright star in Des Moines, Iowa. Colin did everything imaginable to hire the best and the brightest minds in the business. He recruited and imported from anywhere and everywhere at any expense. He paid top dollar and made sure that every engineer was given all the benefits. Colin's philosophy was "You get what you pay for." People were his highest expense. He built the entire reputation of his firm on the experience and quality of his engineers. He believed that if he paid extremely well, nobody would leave.

Then, in 2008, the economy took a turn for the worst. Cashflow became difficult. Colin found himself at the bank borrowing salaries on a routine basis. His engineers were oblivious to the firm's problems and went on with their days in comfort. Finally, Colin's credit ran dry. He was faced with the bitter truth and called the team together to discuss the condition of the company and announce layoffs.

When his employees heard this, they were angry. The ringleader who usually represented the group spoke out.

"Why didn't you tell us that this was happening? We would have much preferred being paid according to how well the company was performing than lose our jobs altogether."

Honesty and transparency are always the best policy when dealing with employees. You will lose them when you lose their trust. Offer Performance Compensation at the time of hire.

Offer one-half of the compensation as a Fixed salary for maintaining the profitability of the position. Offer one-half of the compensation as Semi-Variable Performance Compensation for growing the profitability of the position. When the company does well, everyone does well.

Balance your manager compensation...

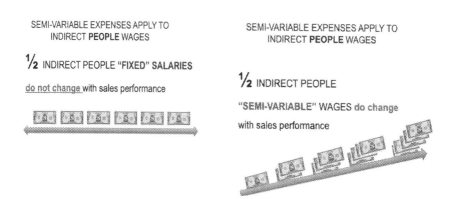

SEMI-VARIABLE EXPENSES APPLY TO INDIRECT **PEOPLE** WAGES

½ INDIRECT PEOPLE "FIXED" **SALARIES**

do not change with sales performance

SEMI-VARIABLE EXPENSES APPLY TO INDIRECT **PEOPLE** WAGES

½ INDIRECT PEOPLE

"SEMI-VARIABLE" WAGES do change

with sales performance

with your Non-People overhead expenses

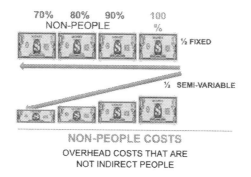

70%   80%   90%   100
NON-PEOPLE   %

½ FIXED

½ SEMI-VARIABLE

NON-PEOPLE COSTS
OVERHEAD COSTS THAT ARE
NOT INDIRECT PEOPLE

In other words, balance equals...

your budgeted Fixed cost items plus the remaining unspent Fixed cost amount in balance with your budgeted Semi-Variable Costs plus the remaining unspent Semi-Variable cost amount. In this way, as costs fluctuate in the year, you do not have to completely re-budget and you always have money to pay your bills.

Adjusting Your Budget Without Re-Budgeting

To manage small fluctuations that occur throughout the year, simply adjust your smaller costs in each budget by using up any unspent costs.

Let's say that your Fixed Non-People Costs include cellphone contracts of $200.

Your Fixed Costs budget for all contracted services has $500 budgeted but still unspent. You want to add another employee to your cellphone contract for $100.

Take $100 from your unspent Fixed Non-People Cost budget and add it to your cell phone contract. Your cellphone contract is adjusted to $300. Your remaining unspent budget is now $400. You may adjust your Fixed budget without increasing it for the year and keep going.

Incidentally, these are all monthly expenses. Large companies usually manage their budgets by the quarter. But all Kanketa small businesses strictly manage by the month.

BALANCE NON-PEOPLE: FIXED & SEMI-VARIABLE

People are easier to balance. Non-People not so much.

This is a graphic illustration of Non-People budget in balance at Normal sales levels. On the LEFT side are the Non-People Fixed Costs. The RIGHT side holds the Non-People Semi-Variable Costs.

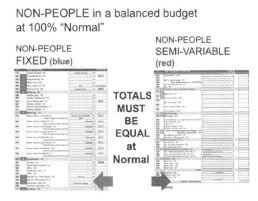

In our example, at 100% Normal the Non-People Costs of $6,000 would be equally divided into $3,000 Fixed Non-People Costs and $3,000 Semi-Variable Non-People Costs.

BALANCE NON-PEOPLE FIXED WITH NON-PEOPLE SEMI-VARIABLE

You must always keep exploring different ways to balance your budget by constantly asking yourself ...

What can I **negotiate?**
What can I **combine?**
What can I **eliminate?**
What can I **outsource?**
What can I **rethink?**
What can I **reassign?**

As you create your budget in this manner, you will find that one and/or both expense sides (Fixed or Semi-Variable Costs) might have an UNSPENT amount of money.

You might also find that one of the sides has a NEGATIVE, or OVERSPENT amount.

When either the Non-People Fixed cost category, or the Non-People Semi-Variable expenses category have money left over after all expenses are budgeted, that category should show the UNSPENT amount.

Budget Overruns

When one side's expenses has a cost overrun and the Fixed or Semi-Variable Costs exceed the budget, that side should show a NEGATIVE or UNSPENT amount.

An unspent part of the budget does not affect the company's balance but, the budget is not in balance when one of the two operational budgets (Fixed or Semi-Variable) exceeds the other.

Different Ways to Say the Same Thing

From time to time, you might find it useful to express your budget as the balance between People (managers) and Non-People.

Your Balanced Budget left is balancing People with Non-People. Your Balanced Budget right is balancing Fixed Costs with Semi-Variable Costs People. It's the same difference.

GROSS SALES at Normal		**GROSS SALES at Normal**	
− cost of goods sold		− cost of goods sold	
_____		_____	
= MARGIN		= MARGIN	
PEOPLE (indirect Managers)	$24,000	**FIXED COSTS**	$24,000
Fixed salaries	$12,000	Fixed People Costs	$12,000
Semi-Variable Performance Compensation	$12,000		
Fixed Non-People Costs	$12,000		
NON-PEOPLE (Operating overhead)		SEMI-VARIABLE COSTS	
		Semi-Variable People Costs	$12,000
Fixed operating costs	$12,000		
Semi-Variable operating costs	$12,000	Semi-Variable Non-People Costs	$12,000
		NET PROFIT	
NET PROFIT − Budget	$24,000	− Budget	$24,000

> The balance between People and Non-People is the same number as the balance between Fixed and Semi-Variable Costs.
> When calculating Net Profit, they are interchangeable.

"FIX IT! DON'T MIX IT."

NEVER PAY FOR NEGATIVE COSTS

in one column with

EXCESS money from another

A big temptation for every business owner is to "rob Peter to pay Paul". It is convenient for a busy owner to take money from one side of the budget to fix the other. This practice of comingling hurts the company in the long run. When you borrow much needed money from the sales budget to pay rent, you are compromising your sales pipeline. When you borrow Semi-Variable car allowances to pay for Fixed insurance premiums, you find yourself visiting your customers less.

Fix the problem with better budgeting, planning and negotiating. Use your line of credit in the way it is intended. If you don't, you will have a hodge-podge of costs that will become uncontrollable. In other words, fix it, don't mix it.

This does completely apply to VARIABLE costs which are Cost of Goods Sold that you don't pay for unless you have work.

The critical balance happens between Fixed Costs (costs that do not change from month to month) and Semi-Variable Costs (costs that do change slightly from month to month by 10% as sales levels increase or decrease.

> **Fix it. Don't Mix it.**
> **Never pay for an overspent (negative) part of the budget on one side of the budget with unspent money from the other side.**

COSTS CAN BE FIXED OR SEMI-VARIABLE ONE YEAR....

AND CHANGE TO THE OTHER THE FOLLOWING YEAR

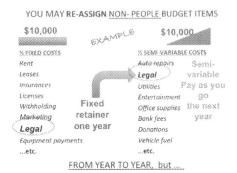

Always work to adjust the budgets to be equal.

Constantly ask yourself …

"What costs can be negotiated to put the cost into the other side?"

"What costs can be combined to put the cost into the other side?"

"What costs can be eliminated or avoided to put the cost into the other side?"

"What costs can be reduced to put the cost into the other side?"

"What costs can be outsourced to put the cost into the other side?"

"What costs can be redesigned, or re-engineer to put the cost into the other side?"

"What costs can be reassigned to put the cost into the other side?"

Make this your money mantra. Do this constantly. Over and over.

It's all about moving expenses from one side to the other to achieve balance.

Take your time with this. Semi-Variable costing will be the key that unlocks your maximum profitability in your business. The goal is to get your Margin to be balanced at various sales performance levels.

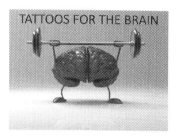

THREE SEMI-VARIABLE TATTOOS FOR THE BRAIN

Here are three main takeaways for the Semi-Variable Costs of a Kanketa Balanced Budget.

#1. Semi-Variable Costs are the backbone of a Balanced Budget. Without Semi-Variable Costs, there is no balance.

#2. Semi-Variable Costs are measured and budgeted in ten percent increments

#3. Semi-Variable cost items can change from year to year, but the 16.67% Semi-Variable budget percent of the Margin remains constant.

True Story: Fix it. Don't Mix it.

The machine shop of Jeremy and Brad in Tuscon, Arizona was always on the fence. Over the years they developed a bad habit of mixing budgets. When they would replace a copier in need of repair by borrowing from the money that was budgeted for a new sales person. They paid for inadequate production space from their customer service budget. They borrowed sales money to pay for delivery from dissatisfied customers. In short, they constantly robbed from both Peter and Paul to pay for some answer that never materialized. Their reasons were always justified by a just-around-the corner sure thing return on investment that was certain to replace the money quickly. The problem escalated when the investments didn't work out as planned.

Finally, they received an offer from a large potential customer. The customer would require more service People than Brad and Jeremy could afford. Unfortunately, the two used the service budget for other things. The customer was not willing to front the machine shop and the customer's opportunity evaporated.

Instead of focusing on better and different possible solutions for the budget insufficiencies and protecting the budget balance, they ignored and upset the critical balance that they needed for long term stability and growth. Had the machine shop kept the budgets separate, they would have been able to take on the new customer who would have paid them enough to fill the financial voids.

CHAPTER 7:

MONEY KEPT

Budget
Parts 7 – 10

NET PROFIT

"How much profit should I make? What's reasonable"
"How much profit am I actually making?"
"If I am making a profit, where is it?"

Whose Net Profit is it, anyway?

Everyone will tell you it's the business owner's Net Profit. Of course, I will agree.

The owner, owns and manages the Net Profit, not the Business Leader (general manager)

It is the owner alone who must decide whether to reinvest in the business, how much and when.

It is the owner alone who must decide whether to put money into savings, how much and when.

It is the owner alone who must decide whether to pay corporate Taxes, how much and when.

It is the owner alone who must decide whether to pay Shareholders, how much and when.

The product of the Kanketa system is not Net Profit. The product of Kanketa is choice. Depending upon the legal structure of the business, the owner might be legally non-compliant by not paying Shareholders or being late on Taxes. There could be interest and penalties at stake. This is no one's business nor responsibility, except that of the business owner.

You are not your business. The business is an EIN number that is separate from the owner and different than the owner's social security number. The business is not unlike someone who owns an apartment building for lease. The business is a system that is capable of making money all by itself when it is in good operating order.

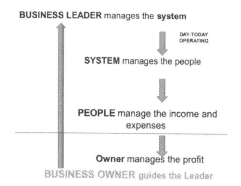

The owner hires a Business Leader and employees to ensure that the business is running by itself on a day-to-day basis in the owner's absence. Right now, you are probably wearing two hats: owner, and Business Leader. The Business Leader might be you.

In most small businesses, the owner is working in the business every day as an employee. However, because the owner still owns the business, the owner must view his/her company like an apartment building. The owner has business upkeep, remodeling, repairs, and Taxes before the owner can put money into their pocket.

The owner hires the building manager in the owner's absence.

In Kanketa ...

- *There is only one Business Leader, hired by the owner*
- *The Business Leader is the general manager.*
- *The Business Leader fully operates the company in the place of the owner*
- *The Business Leader has full check authorization for the budget*
- *Anyone who is assisting the Business Leader is an administrator*
- *The Business Leader is the owner until the owner formally relinquishes full authority*
- *There is no such position as a part time Business Leader*

Without this structure, there is disorganization, confusion, frustrated employees and unnecessary expense.

The owner of the business guides the Business Leader.

The Business Leader is hired to manage the system.

The system manages the People.

The People manage the income and expenses.

The system gives a profit to the owner.

Wash. Rinse. Repeat.

Kanketa's mantra is "Safety first. Profit second." Financial balance leads to business safety.

You are probably under the belief that the whole reason why you are in business is to make as much profit as possible. This depends upon your purpose and definition of "profit."

If you are retired or are on a cruise somewhere for an extended period, wouldn't you rather count on a predictable, set profit coming to you every month, rather than receiving a huge sum one month and nothing the next?

I think so.

THE WORLD OF NET PROFIT

In Kanketa, your Net Profit consists of four equal parts:

1. Money to reinvest into your business to stay competitive
2. Money to put into savings for unforeseen circumstances (business interruptions or opportunities)
3. Money for corporate Taxes
4. Money for you, the owner

This is the only place in the Kanketa system where the word profit is used. Net Profit is what remains of the Margin after all Fixed and Semi-Variable Costs are paid. At least this is what we have been taught. In Kanketa, Net Profit is the first expense to be paid.

More to come on this.

Western business builds budgets from the top down. Kanketa builds budgets from the bottom up. When you put the owner first, the company is really in the first position.

If I were to ask you, "How much should, would, could your business pay you every single month <u>for not showing up</u> while it continues to grow without you?" What would your answer be? Isn't your answer the real reason for owning a business?

I will answer this question in the pages to follow. Certainly, there are a million different reasons to be in your own business. But eventually you will have to sell it, lease it, close it, or give it away. And when you do, it will always come down to money.

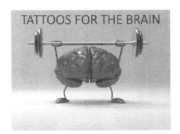

THREE MONEY KEPT TATTOOS FOR THE BRAIN

Here are three main takeaways for money kept in a Kanketa Balanced Budget.

#1. Money Kept is not profit kept.

#2. Money Kept is reliably predictable, sustainable and budgeted for

#3. Money Kept alone does not create personal financial freedom. It is the first step.

True Story: Penny Pinching and Money Kept Are Not Synonymous

The main agenda of the owner of an outdoor power equipment manufacturer in northern Wisconsin was to reduce costs at any expense. The more the company saved, the happier the owner was. The problem was that he pinched every penny until Abraham Lincoln was unrecognizable. The company was extremely profitable in the short term. Budgets were never fully spent. Gradually, the suppliers didn't care if they had his business. Employees were embarrassed to mention that they worked for him.

The word spread to his customers who began to question the value of the product. Finally, whatever was saved in manufacturing expense was eaten up by the constant cost to replace vendors, employees and customers who divorced themselves from the company. Eventually the company shrunk from lack of good, reliable suppliers.

An underspent budget is acceptable when cost reduction is not forced. A Balanced Budget controls the Non-People operating overhead budget parameters so that any unspent amounts in the budget stay in place to become available as the company grows.

An overspent part in a Balanced Budget freezes the entire budget and exposes the issue in real time. Any overspent part of a Balanced Budget demands an immediate resolution. There is no delay, only to discover that the business lost money a month ago.

I often hear owners complain that their business is not profitable. When asked how much they paid themselves from their business account they will always give an amount. So, a more accurate answer is that anyone who took a penny or more from their business made a profit.

In Kanketa, the owner's Net Profit is dependent upon the ability of the Business Leader to keep Fixed and Semi-Variable Costs in balance, but Net Profit is not considered part of the company's available money for operating expenses. The owner of the company may choose to blow it all in Las Vegas over a weekend or reinvest it. How Net Profit is managed is of no concern to the employees of the business or the Business Leader.

The people in the business are hired for only one purpose: to deliver a specific Net Profit to the owner.

HOW BIG SHOULD MY COMPANY BE
IN ORDER TO MAKE THE KIND OF MONEY I WANT?

In the previous chapter, we decided on a better question for owners. "How much could, would, should your business pay you every month for not showing up while it continues to grow without you?"

"Just how much is this?" you ask.

My answer:

#1. Determine the amount of money that you want every month. Make it realistic and assume that you are somewhere in Europe sipping a cool drink, calling back to your office to request spending money for the month.

#2. Multiply this monthly amount by 6 to get the Normal Monthly Margin it will take

(NMM = 100% Normal Monthly Margin).

#3. Add 100% to last year-end total Cost of Goods percent.

#4. Multiply your Normal Monthly Margin (#2 above) by your Cost of Goods percent (#3)

The answer tells you how much your business could, would, and should pay you every month for not showing up while it continues to grow without you.

> **To determine how big your company needs to be, multiply what you want to earn every month times six and add your Cost of Goods Sold. This is your Normal Monthly Gross Sales target.**

True Story: Inventory can keep you from personal financial freedom

John D. operated a shoe distributing company in Sheboygan, Wisconsin. John always claimed that the company rarely made a profit. Yet, John took a significant amount of money out of the company on a routine basis.

Over the years, John reinvested significantly in his company – primarily buying more inventory because he got great deals in quantities. He would defer Taxes and omit paying himself as a Shareholder just to get his hands on more inventory. He believed that inventory was like money in the bank. He wanted to be known to his customers as the distributor with the biggest product choice. Most of all, John believed that his huge inventory was the true value of his company.

As the years went by, John's inventory grew and grew. When John went to sell his company at age 68, the inventory was not selling as fast as it was gathering. Finally, John's inventory caught up with him. He couldn't sell the out-of-stock inventory for what he bought it for. He lost three years of retirement money, over $287,000 which would have been 4 years at $6,000 a month - $72,000 a year of not showing up) trying to give his inventory away.

Focus on growing the Margin year after year. The rest of the 'sure things" are detours.

THE KANKETA PROFIT PLAN

In a high-performing company, Net Profit demands the same balance as all other costs.

Without a defined, written plan, an imbalanced use of Net Profit can create havoc.

The goal for creating Net Profit in a high-performing company:

❖ Consistency
❖ Predictability
❖ Repeatability
❖ Sustainability
❖ Reliability

These goals are not only possible; they are business as usual in Kanketa companies.

After three devastating recalls of hundreds of thousands of vehicles, followed by a tsunami that crippled one-third of Japan, with no bailout government loans, and no employees let go or workforce reduced as a result, why was Toyota in a financial position to show up a week later and advertise aggressively on the Superbowl like nothing happened?

This is because, in a sense, nothing much did happen to Toyota's business. Toyota operates profitably in balance.

NET PROFIT WITHOUT A PLAN

Most of the small business owners I've seen rarely had a concisely followed plan for their profit. They would predictably spend their Net Profit on something unpredictable – often the next shiny object that lands in their path.

NET PROFIT WITH A POOR PLAN

Net Profit can all too easily be spent emotionally. This is usually because small business owners (more predominantly in the U.S.) who are constantly under the pressure of handling day-to-day problems feel that their business owes them. The emotional spending is done without much planning, often in wrong amounts for the wrong reasons.

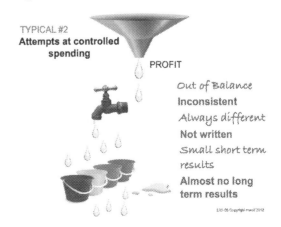

CALCULATING NET PROFIT
IN A BALANCED BUDGET

"How much Net Profit should I make? What's reasonable?"

THE CONCEPT OF SEMI-VARIABLE DOES NOT APPLY TO NET PROFIT. NET PROFIT IS NOT CALCULATED AS A PERCENT OF NORMAL.

When calculating Net Profit, subtract Fixed Costs and Semi-Variable Costs from the Margin in the month's performance column. Net Profit can also be calculated by subtracting People Costs and Non-People Costs from the Margin.

We said earlier that in a Balanced Budget, these cost types are the same numbers.

The Margin of a company in balance has 50% Fixed Costs, and 50% Semi-Variable Costs.
The Margin of a company in balance has 50% People Cost, and 50% Non-People Costs.

It is critical to always remember that the Semi-Variable 10% increase or decrease only applies to operating overhead (employees, and operating costs).

The concept of 10% Semi-Variable increments does **NOT** apply to Net Profit. In other words, if a company performs at 70% of Normal in a month, the Net Profit IS NOT 70% of Net Profit at Normal.

> **The concept of Semi-Variable does not apply to Net Profit. Net Profit is calculated by subtraction. Net Profit is not a percentage of Normal.**

Begin with the four main Net Profit buckets. Divide each equally.

NET PROFIT

25% REINVEST short - long

25% RETAIN short - long

25% TAXES short - long

25% SHAREHOLDERS short - long

REINVEST YOUR NET PROFIT

Never stop reinvesting into your own business. You will always get a better return on your money than from the stock market. However, only invest what you can afford when you can afford it without jeopardizing the other budgets. Your monthly reinvestment budget should not exceed 25% of your total Net Profit.

12.5% Short-term reinvestment – 12 months or less is the expected timeframe that the return on investment should come back to the owner at 3:1 ($3 returned for every dollar invested).

12.5% Long-term reinvestment – 13 months or more is the expected timeframe that the return on investment should come back to the owner at 3:1 ($3 returned for every dollar invested).

SAVE YOUR NET PROFIT
RETAINED EARNINGS (SAVINGS)

Building your corporate savings account is critical to your long-term success for different reasons than you might think. This will be covered in detail. The goal is to become your own bank.

12.5% Short-term Retained Earnings – 12 months or less is the expected timeframe that the profit is used to support potential business problems such as bad debts and business interruptions.

12.5% Long-term Retained Earnings – 13 months or more is the expected timeframe that the profit is used to support unforeseen emergencies.

TAXES –Budget – Part 9 of 10
25% Short-term Tax payments – 12 months or less. The Net Profit from each month builds the corporate tax savings account. On the average, save 17% of Net Profit for federal corporate tax. On the average, save 8% of Net Profit for state corporate tax.

SHAREHOLDERS–Budget – Part 10 of 10
12.5% Shareholder Disbursements – pays Shareholders for the current month.

12.5% is a suggested quarterly distribution.

True Story: Bankrupting with Generosity

Gaylan wanted to reward the employees of this outdoor sporting equipment shop in Dundee, Illinois. He awarded them with stock in the company because they worked hard.

At the end of the year, his intended generosity worked against him. The company wound up at 70% of Normal and the Shareholder Net Profit was very small. Instead of cheers of appreciation, the employees complained. Eventually, they were so disappointed that they banded together and took over Gaylan's company.

It's simple mathematics, and even simpler logic.

DON'T give any employee shares in your company if you can help it. Give them profit-sharing above Normal, which is the only time you can afford it.

DON'T award any employee with shares because they work hard. You are already paying them to work hard and they earn Semi-Variable Performance Compensation for working hard.

If you must give shares (for reasons I am unaware of), don't award more than 19% to any single person. Any employee below 19% is not a significant minority Shareholder.

Only Shareholders with 20% shares or more are considered by banks to be business owners. These are the only acceptable signatures on loans and bank documents.

"How much stock (or shares) should I give to investors?"

Don't add non-participating investors who do not contribute skills and guidance, is the best answer I can give. Accept no passive investors with excuses and stories for why they can't put in more than money. Look closely at what Net Profit you are permanently giving away to a passive investor. You might not have enough profit left to satisfy either of you.

Only if you must:

DEFINE:	10% to the individual who dreamed up the concept of the business
IDENTIFY:	10% to the individual who identified the markets and all resources needed
LOCATE:	10% to the individual who specifically located the markets and the resources needed
QUALIFY:	10% to the individual who contacted the individual resources to understand how the relationship would work (time, team, money)
PROPOSE:	10% to the individual who formalized the key supplier agreements in writing
CLOSE:	10% to the individual who attracts enough potential prospects to launch the business once it's set up
DESIGN:	10% to the individual who designed all work responsibilities for employees and vendors
DEVELOP:	10% to the individual who developed the (written) systems to operate the company
IMPLEMENT:	10% to the individual (Business Leader) who is responsible to carry out the plan and put the systems into profitable action
MANAGE:	10% to the individual who continues to ensure and report progress to the owner of the company

---

= 100% SHAREHOLDER EQUITY

In Kanketa there is no passive money-only investor-shareholders in companies of fewer than 30 employees. Keep your shares. Use your profit to repay a Start-Up loan and avoid passive investors. There are a million less expensive ways to get money besides permanently paying your hard-earned profit to non-participating investors.

"What is my breakeven point?"

When your Kanketa Balanced Budget **is at exactly 50%** of Normal (not 51%) you are at breakeven. Even then, your bills are covered for three months until you figure out how to rescue yourself. Breakeven is the only place where you make absolutely zero dollars of Net Profit (after Breakage).

If you have one dollar or more above exactly 50%, you have made a profit, no matter how small. When your sales fall into the "Zone of Recovery", you are highly dependent upon your balance. This is where Balanced Budgeting becomes critical.

Also, growth – too much or too fast – can push you into the "Zone of Indifference".
This is another danger point since, mathematically you are being drained of cash.
(Hello, Toys-R-Us, Kmart and Sears!).

Zone of Recovery and Zone of Indifference are explained in a later chapter.

> **Kanketa breakeven is exactly 50%**
> **of Net Sales. In Kanketa, the business is**
> **sustainable for three consecutive months**
> **of business interruption**
> **during course correction.**

True Story: Growing too fast is not growing at all

Michael's Y. manufacturing company in Minot, North Dakota produced quality sawblades. He had more orders than is 11 person shop could handle. One day, a global company offered to double his business within six months.

Michael jumped at the chance. His company was already three weeks out in deliveries. He accepted even more orders and his team found themselves working twelve hour days.

Michael was making a good profit but every dime of his profit was being reinvested in Cost of Goods for the new orders. His receivables were further and further out.

Michael was not able to borrow enough to keep up. His delivery times were becoming unreasonably long and the global company was growing increasingly impatient. Finally, production was so late, that the global customer was forced to buy his company just to fulfill its own production commitment.

After 17 years in his own business, Michael ended up with a job at the global company where he works today.

Annual sales growth and consequently Margin increase beyond 20% per year is mathematically not sustainable. Net Profit must always exceed the cost of annual sales growth by no less than one third of annual Margin at 100% Normal.

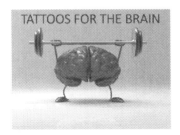

THREE NET PROFIT TATTOOS FOR THE BRAIN

Here are three main takeaways for the Net Profit of a Balanced Budget.

#1. Net Profit is exclusively the owner's money, and exclusively the owner's decision to spend it.

#2. Net Profit has eight equal budget components that should be considered.

#3.Net Profit at each performance level is calculated by subtracting Fixed Costs and Semi-Variable Costs from the Margin. Net Profit is not a percentage of Normal.

CHAPTER 8:

SETTING UP THE BUDGET

"THAT'S A HORRIBLE IDEA.
WHEN DO WE START?"

I'd like to make two comments about using this system.

First: Do not start unless it's a "hell, yes!" If it's not a "hell, yes!" then, it's a "hell, no!"

If you aren't absolutely convinced by now that this approach makes a whole lot of sense, don't go any further. I'm not suggesting that you shouldn't go slowly and carefully. I am suggesting that you should be deliberate. If you live by the belief that whatever got you to this point is no longer sufficient to keep you here, then, proceed vigorously with all determination.

If you are going to proceed, then know that you've already started, and you are half the way there right now. I'm going to walk you step by step through setting up your Balanced Budget by using a reliable tool that you already have in place: your last year's 12 month year-end Profit and Loss statement. It reflects your seasonality and is evidence of what you did naturally to keep your business in place. By simply rearranging your numbers, you will be able to create your Balanced Budget going forward. Once you do, every year thereafter will feed off your starting budget.

When you set up your budget, some minimal **guesswork is initially acceptable** if your business is less than 12 months old.

To set up your budget, put last year's GAAP P&L statement in front of you. Your GAAP P&L does not reflect any kind of balance and it is probably laid out alphabetically.

I will present a first year Start-Up P&L for Larry's Landscaping & Garden Supply. As we work through each of the steps for Larry, apply them to your situation.

Larry's Landscaping & Garden Supply
Profit & Loss
October 2011 through September 2012

	Oct '11 - Sep 12
Ordinary Income/Expense	
Income	
Landscaping Services	57,860.36
Markup Income	815.00
Retail Sales	383.03
Service	6,640.00
Total Income	65,698.39
Cost of Goods Sold	
Cost of Goods Sold	4,220.25
Total COGS	4,220.25
Gross Profit	61,478.14
Expense	
Payroll Expenses	37,820.65
Automobile	738.05
Bank Service Charges	73.50
Delivery Fee	15.00
Insurance	1,835.00
Interest Expense	470.91
Job Expenses	2,427.25
Mileage Reimbursement	0.00
Professional Fees	375.00
Rent	2,400.00
Repairs	45.00
Tools and Misc. Equipment	735.00
Uncategorized Expenses	0.00
Utilities	655.55
Total Expense	47,590.91
Net Ordinary Income	13,887.23
Other Income/Expense	
Other Income	
Misc Income	762.50
Interest Income	91.11
Total Other Income	853.61
Net Other Income	853.61
Net Income	14,740.84

FIG. 8.1

Last year's P&L statement is not your ideal budget by any means – but it is the best hint of where to begin. It gives you hard evidence that you can do a repeat performance and it shows how well you've weathered your sales seasonality.

GET YOUR BALANCE AT NORMAL

Once you have your starting point, it will never again be necessary to look backward. Every year's budget builds on and is managed with the previous year's performance.

BEGIN IN REVIEW:

Kanketa defines Financial Balance as ...

> the point at which
> Fixed Costs, Semi-Variable Costs,
> and Net Profit in the Margin
> are equal.

Kanketa defines Normal Performance as ...

> A monthly budget based on
> the 12 month average of income and expenses
> from the previous tax year.

> Normal is the center of your business's financial universe
> and the starting point for your company's growth.

Larry's P&L that you see here is not the center of Larry's financial universe for his first year in business. Larry is using his GAAP P&L from his 12 months as a place from which to improve.

In the Larry's Landscaping and Garden Supply P&L example, there is no balance between Fixed and Semi-Variable Costs. Larry's company is not safe. The question becomes, what must Larry do to put his business into balance?

Larry's goal is to create a one-time Normal monthly Balanced Budget. Larry wants to know what his monthly sales target must be in order to operate at optimum efficiency with a maximum profit, and without spending one more dime for additional resources.
There are 10 steps that Larry will follow.

Step #1. Identify and Place Any Obvious Job Costs Into Cost of Goods Sold.

The first order of business is to isolate any obvious direct job costs, such as materials and supplies, shipping costs, commissions, etc. that it took to produce and deliver the jobs. These costs are placed into the category of Cost of Goods Sold. These items might already be in the category of Cost of Goods Sold. If so, leave them alone. However, if they are in the section of the P&L under Gross Profit, they should be moved to Cost of Goods Sold.

In Larry's Landscaping example:

	ANNUAL	MONTHLY
Larry's Gross Sales shows		
Landscaping Services	$ 57.880.36	$
Mark Up Income	$ 815.00	$
Retail Sales (Brokered Products)	$ 383.03	$
Service Fees	$ 6,640.00	$
Total Sales of	**$ 65, 698.39**	**$**

FIG. 8.2

Job Expenses

In Larry's expense column under Gross Profit, there is another set of costs generally labeled **job expenses other** for $1,986.11 that belongs to Cost of Goods Sold. Larry has not clearly labeled the Cost of Goods Sold of $4220.25 for materials and supplies.
(FIG. 8.1)

Cost of Quality

Larry explains that he lumped several expenses together including discounts of $ 318.00. to customers. He had also returned product items that were faulty for $123.14. These are called Returns and Allowances on our tax forms. These are Larry's Cost of Quality. It is important to separately track and monitor Cost of Quality. (FIG. 8.1)

Right now, we are unsure as to whether or not the delivery costs of $15.00 in Larry's P&L is for delivering job related items. For budgeting purposes, we will put the $15.00 into Cost of Goods Sold because it will be rare that a business will not have some type of delivery cost during a job.

If we learn that this delivery charge is not job related, we will keep the delivery cost category in Cost of Goods Sold and show $0.00. Then, we will create a separate general delivery charges category in the Gross Profit section.

Larry's Cost of Goods Sold Budget Revised:

GROSS SALES of SERVICES	$	**65,698.35**
returned items	$	123.14
discounts	$	318.00
NET SALES	$	**65,257.21**
COST OF GOODS SOLD		
materials and supplies	$	**4,220.25**
job expenses other	$	**1,986.11**
delivery costs	$	**15.00**
Revised Cost of Goods Sold	$	**6,221.36**

FIG. 8.3

Step #2. Separate Payroll Expense Into Outside Direct Labor Costs (Cost of Goods Sold) and Inside Indirect Manager Salaries

The next order of business is to be clear about direct People Costs and manager costs.

Look for anything in the P&L that suggests payroll. Under Gross Profit in Larry's P&L, there is $37, 820.65 listed as payroll expenses. Mixed into Larry's payroll expenses in the Gross Profit section is a sub-contracted direct labor worker who was paid hourly to do landscaping for a total of $7,820.65 for the year.

Larry should have paid this person as a 1099 sub-contractor for outside direct labor for contracted services in Cost of Goods Sold, and not mixed this person with his manager payroll expense in the Gross Profit. From Larry's gross payroll of $37,820.65 on his P&L statement, Larry will subtract $7,820.65 for his subcontractor and add this amount to his Cost of Goods Sold. Larry's gross payroll in his Gross Profit at this point is now **$51,215.20**

Larry's Budget Revised:	ANNUAL	MONTHLY	
		(12 month average)	
GROSS SALES	**$ 65,698.35**	**$ 5,474.86**	
minus returned items	$ 123.14		
minus discounts	$ 318.00		
NET SALES	**$ 65,257.21**	**$ 5,438.10**	
COST OF GOODS SOLD			
contracted labor	**$ 7,820.65**	**$ 650.00**	
materials and supplies	$ 4,220.25	$ 351.69	
job expenses other	$ 1,986.11	$ 165.51	
delivery costs	$ 15.00		
Revised Cost of Goods Sold	**$ 14,042.01**		
REVISED GROSS PROFIT	**$ 51,215.20**	**$ 4,270.00**	FIG. 8.4

Remember that we are calling Gross Profit the "Margin." After subtracting the $ 7,820.65 for outside contracted labor from Larry's payroll expenses, Larry will use the $30,000 balance of his payroll budget as his gross payroll for his manager and himself. Larry isn't including any benefits at this time.

Payroll Expenses

Larry has a part time manager in the company who supervises all jobs. Larry pays the manager $1,500 a month to show up whether the company has work or not. The manager is not contracted hourly by the job, and makes a salary for showing up every day to work on all jobs. The manager does administrative work when he is not out in the field.

Larry's Revised Budget with his Payroll Expense added:

	ANNUAL	MONTHLY (rounded)
GROSS SALES	**$ 65,698.35**	**$ 5,474.86**
returned items	$ 123.14	
discounts	$ 318.00	
NET SALES	**$ 65,257.21**	**$5,438.10**
COST OF GOODS SOLD		
contracted labor	**$ 7,820.65**	**$ 650.00**
materials and supplies	$ 4,220.25	$ 351.69
job expenses other	$ 1,986.11	$ 165.50
delivery costs	$ 15.00	
Revised Cost of Goods Sold	**$ 14,042.01**	
GROSS PROFIT	**$ 51,215.20**	**$ 4,270.00**
Larry's Actual		
Cost of Goods Sold	**$14,042.01**	**$ 1,170.00**
MARGIN	**$51,215.20**	**$ 4,270.00**
People Costs (Payroll)		
Manager 1 (part time)	$18,000.00	$ 1,500.00

FIG. 8.5

Step #3. Determine What the Owner (Larry) Does While Working In the Business.

Larry works in his business as a landscape designer. He is also the manager of the company.

Payroll and expense laws are different with the various types of legal structures.

In a Sub-S Corporation, the owner must be a salaried employee up to 500 hours a year.

Larry must pay himself a salary as a manager working 500 hours a year in his business. After paying $18,000 to his part-time manager, Larry has $12,000 left for his payroll. This amount includes withholding Taxes. Larry is paying himself $1,000 a month as a marketing and sales manager who works with customers on their designs.

	ANNUAL	MONTHLY (rounded)
GROSS SALES	$ 65,698.35	$ 5,474.86
returned items	$ 123.14	
discounts	$ 318.00	
NET SALES	$ 65,257.21	$5,438.10
COST OF GOODS SOLD		
contracted labor	$ 7,820.65	$ 650.00
materials and supplies	$ 4,220.25	$ 351.69
job expenses other	$ 1,986.11	$ 165.51
delivery costs	$ 15.00	
Cost of Goods Sold	$ 14,042.01	
MARGIN	$ 51,215.20	$ 4,270.00
People Costs (Payroll)		
Manager 1 (part time)	$ 18,000.00	$ 1,500.00
People Costs (Payroll)		
Manager 1 (part time)	$ 18,000.00	$ 1,500.00
Manager 1 (Larry's salary)	$ 12,000.00	$ 1,000.00
People costs (managers)	$ 30,000.00	$ 2,500.00

FIG. 8.6

These payroll amounts are pre-tax and include payroll withholding. If an outside payroll company is used, the total payroll and withholding will come out of the bank at the same time as gross wages and won't be separated.

Step #4. Subtract all People Costs (manager payroll) from the Total Margin (Gross Profit) to find the budget for Non-People Costs and Net Profit.

	ANNUAL	MONTHLY (rounded)
GROSS SALES	**$ 65,698.35**	**$ 5,474.86**
returned items	$ 123.14	
discounts	$ 318.00	
NET SALES	**$ 65,257.21**	**$5,438.10**
COST OF GOODS SOLD		
contracted labor	**$ 7,820.65**	**$ 650.00**
materials and supplies	$ 4,220.25	$ 351.69
job expenses other	$ 1,986.11	$ 165.51
delivery costs	$ 15.00	
Cost of Goods Sold	**$ 14,042.01**	
MARGIN	**$ 51,215.20**	**$ 4,270.00**
People Costs (Payroll)		
Manager 1 (part time)	$ 18,000.00	$ 1,500.00
People Costs (Payroll)		
Manager 1 (part time)	$ 18,000.00	$ 1,500.00
Manager 1 (Larry's salary)	$ 12,000.00	$ 1,000.00
People costs (managers)	**$ 30,000.00**	**$ 2,500.00**

Margin $51,215.20 - People Costs of $30,000 = Non-People Costs

Non-People Costs	**$21,215.20**	**$1,770.00**

Operating overhead to run the company
plus Net Profit

FIG. 8.7

Step #5: Find the NORMAL BALANCED MONTHLY MARGIN

To find the this year's annual 12-month balanced <u>MARGIN</u> budget at Normal, multiply the <u>LARGEST</u> of last year's People Costs (manager wages) and Non-People Costs by 3

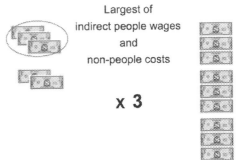

Largest of
indirect people wages
and
non-people costs

x 3

Larry's MARGIN Budget:

LARRY's PEOPLE COSTS

People Costs (Payroll)

Manager 1 (part time)	$18,000.00	$1,500.00
Manager 2 (Larry's salary)	$12,000.00	$1,000.00
People Costs	**$30,000.00**	
Non-People Costs	**$21,215.20**	**$1,770.00**

FIG. 8.8

Operating overhead to run the company plus Net Profit

Larry will use his annual $30,000 People Costs for this.

$30,000 X 3 = $90,000

Larry's 12 month Margin budget
at 100% Normal Performance

Step #6. Establish the NEW NORMAL BALANCED BUDGET

Separate the New Normal Margin budget into 3 EQUAL parts.

It is necessary for Larry to take the balancing act one step further by creating a balanced Margin budget at 100% Normal. Larry must separate the Fixed Costs that do not change every month from the Semi-Variable Costs that will change slightly with the performance of the business.

Fixed Costs that do not change from month to month

	ANNUAL	MONTHLY
Fixed cost budget at 100% Normal: 1/3 of $ 90,000	$ 30,000	$2,500

Semi-Variable Costs that do change from month to month

	ANNUAL	MONTHLY
Semi-Variable cost budget at 100% Normal: 1/3 of $ 90,000	$ 30,000	$2,500
Net Profit budget at 100% Normal: 1/3 of $ 90,000	$ 30,000	$2,500

FIG. 8.9

Step #7. Separate the 3 Main Budget Sections Into...

Fixed People and Non-People Costs

Semi-Variable People Costs and Semi-Variable Non-People Costs

Net Profit will follow.

Larry's Revised Margin Budget:

	ANNUAL	MONTHLY (Adjusted)
MARGIN @ Normal	$90,000.00	$ 30,000
FIXED COST BUDGET @ Normal	$30,000.00	$ 2,500
Fixed People Costs – manager salaries	$15,000.00	$ 1,250
Fixed Non-People Cost – overhead	$15,000.00	$ 1,250
SEMI-VARIABLE COST BUDGET @ Normal	$30,000.00	$ 2,500
Semi-Variable People Costs manager Performance Compensation	$15,000.00	$ 1,250
Semi-variable Non-People Costs	$15,000.00	$ 1,250
NET PROFIT BUDGET @ Normal	$30,000.00	$ 2,500

FIG. 8.10

Step #8. Place All Actual Costs From the Gross Profit Section of Your P&L Into the Appropriate People and Non-People Sections of Your New Margin Budget.

Larry's People Costs P&L actual - placed into his Margin:

	ANNUAL	MONTHLY
PEOPLE COSTS		
Larry's People Costs (Payroll)		
Manager 1 (part time)	$ 18,000.00	$ 1,500.00
Manager 1 (Larry's salary)	$ 12,000.00	$ 1,000.00
People costs (managers)	**$ 30,000.00**	**$ 2,500.00**
NON-PEOPLE COSTS		
Larry's Non-People Overhead		
Automobile gas and oil	$ 738.05	$ 61.50
Bank Service charge	$ 73.50	$ 6.13
FUTA SUTA FICA Tax matching 17.65	$ 5,295.00	$ 441.25
Insurance	$ 1,835.00	$ 152.92
Interest	$ 470.88	$ 39.24
Mileage reimbursement	$ 0.00	$ 0.00
Professional fees	$ 375.00	$ 31.25
Rent	$ 2,400.00	$ 200.00
Repairs	$ 45.00	$ 3.75
Tools and miscellaneous	$ 735.00	$ 61.25
Utilities	$ 655.55	$ 54.63
Larry's Actual Non-People Costs	**$ 12,637.43**	**$ 1,052.12**

FIG. 811

Step #9. Balance Non-People Costs Further

Separate all actual Non-People Fixed Costs from actual Non-People Semi-Variable Costs.

Larry's actual Non-People Fixed Costs
Operating Overhead

FUTA SUTA FICA Tax matching 17.65	$ 5,295.00	$ 441.25
Insurance	$ 1,835.00	$ 152.92
Interest	$ 470.88	$ 39.24
Rent	$ 2,400.00	$ 200.00
Total Non-People Fixed Costs:	**$ 10,000.88**	**$ 833.41**

Larry's actual Non-People Semi-Variable Costs

Automobile gas and oil	$ 738.05	$ 61.50
Bank Service charge	$ 73.50	$ 6.13
Mileage reimbursement	$ 0.00	$ 0.00
Professional fees	$ 375.00	$ 31.25
Repairs	$ 45.00	$ 3.75
Tools and miscellaneous	$ 735.00	$ 61.25
Utilities	$ 655.55	$ 54.63
Total Non-People Semi-Variable Costs:	**$ 2,622.10**	**$ 218.50**

FIG. 812

Step #10. Add an UNSPENT COST Line To Each of the Four Expense Budgets:

Fixed People Costs Unspent
Fixed Non-People Costs Unspent
Semi-Variable People Costs Unspent
Semi-Variable Non-People Costs Unspent

DO NOT EXCEED THESE BUDGETS
Only go up to the Fixed People Costs limit.

Larry's actual Non-People Fixed Costs
Operating Overhead

FUTA SUTA FICA Tax matching 17.65	$ 5,295.00	$ 441.25
Insurance	$ 1,835.00	$ 152.92
Interest	$ 470.88	$ 39.24
Rent	$ 2,400.00	$ 200.00
Total Non-People Fixed Costs:	**$ 10,000.88**	**$ 833.41**
People Costs Budget	**$ 15,000.00**	
UNSPENT	**$ 4,999.12**	

Over/Under Budget Non-People Fixed Costs

Larry's actual Non-People Semi-Variable Costs

Automobile gas and oil	$ 738.05	$ 61.50
Bank Service charge	$ 73.50	$ 6.13
Mileage reimbursement	$ 0.00	$ 0.00
Professional fees	$ 375.00	$ 31.25
Repairs	$ 45.00	$ 3.75
Tools and miscellaneous	$ 735.00	$ 61.25
Utilities	$ 655.55	$ 54.63
Total Non-People Semi-Variable Costs:	**$ 2,622.10**	**$ 218.50**
Non-People Semi-Variable Costs Budget	**$ 15,000.00**	
UNSPENT	**$ 12,377.90**	

Over/Under Budget Non-People Fixed Costs

FIG. 813

Step #11. Put the Amount of All Non-People Fixed Costs (That Exceed the People Fixed Budget) Into People Semi-Variable.

Make Fixed People Costs equal to each other.
Make People Over/Under Budget Fixed People Costs a zero.

WAS:

	ANNUAL	MONTHLY
100% People Fixed Costs (Payroll)		
Manager 1 (part time)	$ 18,000.00	$ 1,500.00
Manager 2 (Larry's salary)	$ 12,000.00	$ 1,000.00
Larry's Actual People Costs	**$ 30,000.00**	**$ 2,500.00**

IS NOW (IN BALANCE):

	ANNUAL	MONTHLY
50% People Fixed Costs (Payroll)		
Manager 1 (part time)	$ 7,500.00	$ 1,250.00
Manager 2 (Larry's salary)	$ 7,500.00	$ 1,250.00
Larry's Revised Fixed People Costs	**$ 15,000.00**	**$ 1,250.00**
UNSPENT	**$ 0.00**	
Over/Under Budget Fixed People Costs	**$ 0.00**	

50% People Semi-Variable Costs (Performance Compensation at Normal)

	ANNUAL	MONTHLY
Manager 1(part time) Performance Compensation at Normal)	$ 7,500.00	$ 625.00
Manager 2 (Larry's Performance Compensation at Normal)	$ 7,500.00	$ 625.00
Larry's Actual Semi-Variable People Costs	**$ 15,000.00**	**$ 1,250.00**
UNSPENT	**$ 0.00**	
Over/Under Budget Semi-Variable People Costs	**$ 0.00**	

FIG. 814

Step #12. Do Not Touch Any Over-Budgeted Non-People Costs That Exceed the Non-People Fixed and Semi-Variable Budget. Show Them As NEGATIVE UNSPENT

EXAMPLE:

Larry's Tool Costs and other Miscellaneous Items pushed his NON-PEOPLE FIXED COSTS Over Budget

If Larry's P&L Non-People Fixed Costs Actuals were Over Budget, Larry's Operating Overhead would look like this:

Automobile gas and oil	$	738.05	$	61.50
Bank Service charge	$	73.50	$	6.13
Mileage reimbursement	$	0.00	$	0.00
Professional fees	$	375.00	$	31.25
Repairs	$	45.00	$	3.75
➤ **TOOLS & MISCELLANEOUS**	**$**	**13,850**	**$**	
Utilities	$	655.55	$	54.63
Total Actual Non-People Semi-Variable Costs:	**$ 15,737.10**		**$1,311.43**	
Larry's People Costs Budget UNSPENT	**$ 15,000.00**		**$2,500.00**	
Over/Under Budget Semi-Variable Non-People Costs	**<$**	**737.10>**	**<$**	**61.43>**

What can be done to re-negotiate these so that the budget is not overspent?

FIG. 815

Step #13. Review All Budget Items For Discrepancies

Fixed People Costs

The Fixed People budget for salaries should always be used to pay whomever is working as Indirect managers in the company.

Larry's Oversites in Fixed Non-People Costs:
After a closer look at Larry's Non-People budget, there are two Fixed items missing:
a Fixed cellphone contract that Larry pays every month, and a Fixed, recurring monthly software lease payment. Larry added these to his budget.

Larry's Semi-Variable People Costs
In the first year of business Larry's business performance is his 100% starting point. He paid his manager the full performance pay. Because of poor cashflow Larry underpaid his own Performance Compensation by $2,000. If Larry had an adequate Line of Credit, this would not have been necessary.

Oversites in Semi-Variable Non-People Costs
In Semi-Variable Non-People Costs, Larry overlooked office supplies, and the cash that he gave to his manager as re-imbursement for visiting customers. He also forgot to budget the lunches he bought for customers and the three industry tradeshows that Larry attended during the year.

	ANNUAL	MONTHLY (Adjusted)
FIXED Non-People Overhead		
➢ *(added) Cellphone monthly contract*	$ 720.00	$ 60.00
FUTA SUTA FICA Tax matching 17.65	$ 5,295.00	$ 441.25
Insurance	$ 1,835.00	$ 152.92
Interest	$ 470.88	$ 39.24
Rent	$ 2,400.00	$ 200.00
➢ *(added) Software license*	$ 600.00	$ 50.00
Initial Fixed Non-People Costs:	$ 10,000.88	$ 833.40
Added to the Budget	$ 1,320.00	$ 110.01
Revised Total Fixed Non-People Costs:	$ 11,320.88	$ 943.41

	ANNUAL	MONTHLY
SEMI-VARIABLE Non-People Costs		
Automobile gas and oil	$ 738.05	$ 61.50
Bank Service charge	$ 73.50	$ 6.13
➤ *(added) Meals and entertainment*		
	$ 212.00	*$ 17.67*
➤ *(added) Mileage reimbursement*		
Employees	*$ 576.00*	*$ 48.00*
Professional fees	$ 375.00	$ 31.25
➤ *(added) Office supplies*	*$ 672.00*	*$ 56.00*
Repairs	$ 45.00	$ 3.75
Tools and miscellaneous	$ 735.00	$ 61.25
➤ *(added) Training Seminars*	*$ 3,041.35*	*$ 253.45*
Utilities	$ 655.55	$ 54.63

Initial Semi-Variable Non-People Costs:	**$ 2,622.10**	**$ 218.50**
Items Added to the Budget	**$ 4,501.35**	**$ 375.11**
Revised Semi-Variable Non-People:	**$ 7,123.45**	**$ 593.62**

FIG. 8.16

Step #14. Divide the 1/3 Budgeted Net Profit at Normal Into Its Eight Equal Net Profit Components.

Here is what Larry's new monthly Net Profit budget now looks like at Normal:

	ANNUAL	MONTHLY
1/3 NET PROFIT AT NORMAL	$ 10,000.00	$ 104.17 at Normal
12.5% of Net Profit Larry's budget for reinvestment *short term*:	$ 1,250 at Normal	$ 104.17 at Normal
12.5% of Net Profit Larry's budget for reinvestment *long term*:	$ 1,250 at Normal	$ 104.17 at Normal
12.5% of Net Profit Larry's budget for Retained Earnings *short term*:	$ 1,250 at Normal	$ 104.17 at Normal
12.5% of Net Profit Larry's budget for Retained Earnings l*ong term:*	$ 1,250 at Normal	$ 104.17 at Normal
25% of Budgeted Net Profit 17% budget for federal corporate Taxes:	$ 1,700 at Normal	$ 141.67 at Normal
8% budget for state corporate Taxes:	$ 800 at Normal	$ 66.67 at Normal
25% of Net Profit Budget for Shareholder dividends	$ 1,250 at Normal	$ 104.17 at Normal
Budget for Shareholder dividends	$ 1,250	$ 104.17

FIG. 8.17

Step #15. Add The Newly Adjusted Cost of Goods Sold
In Steps 1-3, Adjustments were made to last year's Cost of Goods Sold

ADD THE ADJUSTED COST OF GOODS SOLD AMOUNT TO THE NEW MARGIN AT NORMAL
to find this year's Normal Gross Sales target

Larry realizes that, so far, he didn't add the Cost of Goods Sold yet.
In Steps 1 and 2 Larry added contracted labor and delivery costs to last year's P&L.

	ANNUAL	MONTHLY
NEW SALES TARGET AT 100% NORMAL (adjusted)	$ 104,042.01	$ 8,670.17
Cost of Goods Sold (adjusted in Steps 1-3)	$ 14,042.01	$ 1,170.00
MARGIN @ Normal	$ 90,000.00	$ 7,500.00

FIG. 8.18

Larry's will add his adjusted Cost of Goods Sold for last year of $14,042 to his current Normal Balanced Margin:

Step #16. FIND THE CENTER OF YOUR FINANCIAL UNIVERSE

All of Larry's costs line up perfectly and the budget is in balance, with three small adjustments.

- Remove the pennies throughout
  Gross Sales - $ 104,042

- Round the Gross Sales performance up or down to the nearest $5,000.

  NEW SALES TARGET AT 100% NORMAL

  $ 104,042.01 rounded to $ 105,000 (The Center of Larry's Financial Universe)

- Add the difference between the Budgeted Gross Sales amount and the rounded final amount to Cost of Quality.

  $ 105,000 minus $104,042 = $ 958
  In Larry's case, he will add $958 to his Cost of Quality Budget

  The 100% Normal Balanced Budget of $105,000 for the current year through December 31 will be the basis for all of Larry's financial decisions

  More to come in the next Chapter – the "Scorecard"

Organize Your P&L to Match the Budget

Ideally, your P&L should be organized so that you can clearly see the ten main kanketa budget categories that include every expense in your business.

Separate every single cost item on your P&L into your main buckets.

The primary expense categories, Fixed and Semi-Variable, will align with your tax return. Larry's first year P&L does not reflect balance. This is quite understandable. Most Start-Ups that have no concept of Balanced Budgeting take a lot longer to develop than is necessary.

Have your accountant organize a report showing the main categories of your Kanketa Balanced Budget.

	Sales Mgr. Fixed Wages	Employee Wages	500
6103	Velocity Mgr. Fixed Wages	Employee Wages	500
	HR Ldrshp Mgr. Fixed Wages	Employee Wages	500
6104	Customer Srvc Mgr. Fixed Wages	Employee Wages	500
	Customer Care Mgr. Fixed Wages	Employee Wages	500
6105	Administration Fixed Wages	Employee Wages	500
6106	Business Leader Fixed Wages	Employee Wages	500

6200 - 6299 FIXED PEOPLE COSTS - EMPLOYEE BENEFITS

6200 Group Benefits	Employee Benefits	
6201 Product Mgr. Benefits	Employee Benefits	
Production Mgr. Benefits	Employee Benefits	
6202 Marketing Mgr. Benefits	Employee Benefits	
Sales Mgr. Benefits	Employee Benefits	
6203 Velocity Mgr. Benefits	Employee Benefits	
HR Ldrshp Mgr. Benefits	Employee Benefits	
6204 Customer Srvc Mgr. Benefits	Employee Benefits	
Customer Care Mgr. Benefits	Employee Benefits	
6205 Administration Benefits	Employee Benefits	
6206 Business Leader Benefits	Employee Benefits	

6300-6399 FIXED NON-PEOPLE COSTS

6301 - 6309	**ADVERTISING**	**Non-people Fixed**	560
6301	Attended Events	Non-people Fixed	
6302	Displays	Non-people Fixed	
6303	Print	Non-people Fixed	
6304	Radio/ Television	Non-people Fixed	
6305	Social Media	Non-people Fixed	
6306	Wearables	Non-people Fixed	
6307	Website Service - Maintenance	Non-people Fixed	
6308 - 6309	Advertising - Other	Non-people Fixed	567
6320 - 6329	**INSURANCE**	**Non-people Fixed**	
	General Business Liability		
	Property Insurance	Non-people Fixed	618
	Vehicle Insurance	Non-people Fixed	615
	Workman's Comp	Non-people Fixed	617
6330 - 6339	**CONTRACTS - Monthly**	**Non-people Fixed**	
6330	Cell Phone	Non-people Fixed	
6331	Landline	Non-people Fixed	
6332	Cleaning - Janitorial Services	Non-people Fixed	583
6333	Dues and Subscriptions	Non-people Fixed	550
6334	Internet Service	Non-people Fixed	565
6335	Security	Non-people Fixed	

FIG. 8.19

Which financial picture do you think Larry will find more useful, Larry's original P&L here, or Larry's Kanketa Balanced Budget? Which helps Larry the most to make good day-to-day decisions?

Larry's Landscaping & Garden Supply
Profit & Loss
October 2011 through September 2012

	Oct '11 - Sep 12
Ordinary Income/Expense	
Income	
Landscaping Services	57,860.36
Markup Income	815.00
Retail Sales	383.03
Service	6,640.00
Total Income	65,698.39
Cost of Goods Sold	
Cost of Goods Sold	4,220.25
Total COGS	4,220.25
Gross Profit	61,478.14
Expense	
Payroll Expenses	37,820.65
Automobile	738.05
Bank Service Charges	73.50
Delivery Fee	15.00
Insurance	1,835.00
Interest Expense	470.91
Job Expenses	2,427.25
Mileage Reimbursement	0.00
Professional Fees	375.00
Rent	2,400.00
Repairs	45.00
Tools and Misc. Equipment	735.00
Uncategorized Expenses	0.00
Utilities	655.55
Total Expense	47,590.91
Net Ordinary Income	13,887.23
Other Income/Expense	
Other Income	
Misc Income	762.50
Interest Income	91.11
Total Other Income	853.61
Net Other Income	853.61
Net Income	14,740.84

(FIG. 8.1)

GOLDERN RULE: Do anything you want. Just stay within the Balanced Budget and do it safely.

Make Any Budget Adjustments To Your Budget at Normal

For example, if cellphones in your Semi-Variable budget are averaging $150 a month, and climb to $180 a month as a trend average, you should first try to lower another expense in your Semi-Variable budget by $30.

When you see that $180 is a trend and generally a stable new expense for cellphones, look for unspent money in the Semi-Variable portion of your budget.

Always use your budget at Normal to maintain and adjust any Fixed vs. Semi-Variable cost changes.

MORE THAN 20% ANNUAL SALES GROWTH OVER THE PRIOR YEAR'S NORMAL IS RISKY BUSINESS

"What should I target for reasonable business growth?"

More than 20% sales growth is not sustainable. This 20% rule assumes that the company its money and resources to the fullest level.

Mathematically, 20% is the maximum safe, growth that is sustainable per year for a small business. More than this growth level will send the company on a downward trajectory that will create a cash flow problem and send it out of balance.

Sales growth demands cash flow. Growth rates are directly proportionate to debt.

If a company grows 30% per year (10% more than the recommended maximum), there is a proportionate cash depletion.

Kanketa metrics – "Ketalytics" are used to predict the month that the company must stop growing and recover, or it will be traumatized.

It would be better to maintain safe performance levels with this company, and buy another company, or start a division with a different budget.

Kanketa defines growth as a widening of Margin by balancing increases of revenue on the right side of the house with debt reductions on the left side of the house.

GOOD PRACTICE #1: NEVER sacrifice balance for employee pay. If you do, you might set yourself up for non-recoverable imbalance later.

GOOD PRACTICE #2: NEVER take money away from an employee. They will quit, and can create more harm to your reputation than you may be able to defend

GOOD PRACTICE #3: NEVER pay a manager for more than a one Workroom employee, even temporarily. You will not have enough money to hire the Real McCoy later without taking away the compensation of the temporary employee.

The Balance Between Health and Safety

In my books "I Used to Love My Business. Now I Hate It," and "The Most Critical Number In Your Business (Is Not Net Profit)". I presented how your Debt-To-Income ratio (DTI) measures and manages your company's health.

However, a Balanced Budget manages your company's safety. You can be in great health and walk out onto the street and a car can run over your toes. You can be safe inside your house and be in poor health with the flu. When it's in balance, your company will have a strong immune system and **be sheltered from the elements.**

Debt-to-Income ratio measures the
company's health.
The balance between Fixed and
Semi-Variable Costs measures
the company's safety.

STANDARD WORK
Setting Up Your Balanced Budget For The First Time

Step #1. Identify and place any obvious job costs into Cost of Goods Sold.

Step #2. Separate payroll expense into outside direct labor costs (Cost of Goods Sold) and inside indirect manager salaries

Step #3. Determine what the owner (Larry) does while working in the business

Step #4. Subtract all People Costs (manager payroll) from the total Margin (Gross Profit) to find the budget for Non-People Costs and Net Profit.

Step #5: Find the NORMAL BALANCED MONTHLY MARGIN

Step #6. Establish the new Kanketa Normal Balanced Budget

Step #7. Separate the 3 main budget sections

Step #8. Place all actual costs from the Gross Profit section of your P&L into the appropriate People and Non-People sections of your new Margin budget.

Step #9. Balance People Costs further.

Step #10. Add an UNSPENT COST line to each of the four budgets:

Step #11. Put the amount of all People Costs that exceed the Fixed People Budget into People Semi-Variable.

Step #12. DO NOT TOUCH ANY OVER-BUDGETED NON-PEOPLE COSTS

Step #13. Review all budget items for discrepancies

Step #14. Divide the 1/3 Budgeted Net Profit at Normal Into Its eight equal Net Profit components.

Step #15. Add the newly adjusted Cost of Goods Sold to the new Margin

Step #16. FIND THE CENTER OF YOUR FINANCIAL UNIVERSE

"But wait!. There's a problem!"

Some of you might be thinking…

*"**We don't sell at this new performance level. Our Gross Sales last year were significantly less than this new Normal target. Our whole budget is less. The numbers don't work"***

DIVIDE LAST YEAR'S GROSS SALES
BY THIS YEAR'S NEW SALES TARGET.
TO GET THE CURRENT PERFORMANCE
PERCENTAGE THAT YOUR COMPANY
IS CURRENTLY PERFORMING AGAINST ITS
OPTIMUM POTENTIAL

In Larry's case, this year's 12 month Normal Gross Sales target of $105,000, divided by last year's Gross Sales of $65,698, gives Larry a current performance percentage of 63%.

In other words, Larry is only getting a 63% return on his assets.

Larry's efficiency of 63% means that he can redirect his People and Non-People Costs and improve the use of his Net Profit by another 37%.

So, what are we are we saying here?

With Larry's current resources, if managed correctly, Larry should be able to produce $105,000. This also means that he is probably underspending available money in certain areas of his business.

For clarification, Larry's 37% is not risky (more than annual sales growth over prior year's Normal). The 20% rule assumes that the company is using its money and resources to their fullest. Larry's company isn't.

FOLLOW THE BUDGET CONTOUR

	LARRY'S ACTUAL SALES PERFORMANCE LAST YEAR	LARRY'S POTENTIAL SALES WITH FULL USE HIS RESOURCES
GROSS SALES **NET SALES** (1% of Gross Sales for Larry)	$ 65,698	$ 105,000
After Returns and Allowances (Includes the difference of $ 958 when sales are rounded. See Step #16)	$ 65,257	$ 103,950
COST OF GOODS SOLD	$ 14,042 (21.4% of Normal Gross Sales for Larry)	$ 14,042 (13.4% of Normal Gross Sales for Larry)
MARGIN (Net Sales minus minus Cost of Goods Sold)	$ 51,215	$ 90,000 ($89,908 Rounded to $90,000)
PEOPLE COSTS		
Fixed Costs (Payroll)	50% of People Budget at Normal	50% of People Budget at Normal
Manager 1 (part time)	$ 7,500	$ 7,500
Manager 2 (Larry's salary)	$ 7,500	$ 7,500
Larry's Fixed People Costs	$ 15,000	$ 15,000
Over/Under Budget Fixed **People Costs**	$ 0	$ 0

FIG. 8.20

Fixed costs do not change from month to month. Larry would pay the same fixed salaries

At 100% or 63% performance.

People Semi-Variable Costs
(Performance Compensation at Normal)

Semi-Variable costs DO change from month to month.
Larry would pay a Performance Compensation based on 63%.

	At 63% Normal Larry's Current Performance Compensation	At 100% Normal Larry's Potential Performance Compensation
Manager 1 (part time)	$ 4,720	$ 7,500
Manager 2 (Larry's salary)	$ 4,720	$ 7,500
Larry's Semi-Variable People Costs	**$ 9,440**	**$ 15,000**

Margin - People Costs = Non-People Costs

Larry's Margin of $51,215
minus – Larry's People Costs at 63%
(Fixed Costs of $ 15,000 and Semi-Variable Costs of $9,440)

FIG. 8.21

NON-PEOPLE COSTS

Non-People Fixed Costs	Non-People Budget at 63% of Normal	50%ofNon-People Budget at 100% of Normal
Larry's Fixed Non-People Costs	$ 7,500	$ 7,500
Over/Under Budget Fixed Non-People Costs	$ 0	$ 0

FIG. 8.22

Larry would pay the same fixed costs at 100% or 63% performance.

Non-People Semi-Variable Costs

Semi-Variable costs DO change from month to month.
Larry would pay a Performance Compensation based on 63%.

	At 63% Normal Larry's Current Non-People Semi-Variable Budget	At 100% Normal Larry's Potential Semi-Variable Costs
Semi-Variable Non-People Costs	$ 9,440	$ 15,000

FIG. 8.32

NET PROFIT

Margin minus People Costs minus Non-People Costs
equals Net Profit

Larry's Margin of $51,215
minus – Larry's People Costs
(Fixed Costs of $ 15,000 and Semi-Variable Costs of $9,440)

Balance $26,775

minus – Larry's Non-People Costs at 63%
(Fixed Costs of $ 15,000 and Semi-Variable Costs of $9,440)

Balance $2,334

At 63% Normal Larry's Current NET PROFIT	At 100% Normal Larry's Potential NET PROFIT
1/3 $2,334	1/3 $30,000

At 63% Normal   At 100% Normal

NET PROFIT	Larry's Current NET PROFIT of $2,334	Larry's Potential NET PROFIT of 1/3 $30,00 at Normal
12.5% of Net Profit Larry's budget for Reinvestment *short term:*	$ 292 at Normal	$ 3,750 at Normal
12.5% of Net Profit Larry's budget for Reinvestment *long term*:	$ 292 at Normal	$ 3,750 at Normal
12.5% of Net Profit Larry's budget for Retained Earnings *short term*:	$ 292 at Normal	$ 3,750 at Normal
12.5% of Net Profit Larry's budget for Retained Earnings l*ong term:*	$ 292 at Normal	$ 3,750 at Normal
25% of Budgeted Net Profit 17% budget for federal corporate Taxes:	$ 396.78 at Normal	$ 5,100 at Normal
8% budget for state corporate Taxes:	$ 186.72 at Normal	$ 2,400 at Normal
25% of Net Profit Budget for Shareholder dividends	$ 584 at Normal	$ 7,500 at Normal

FIG. 8.24

This disparity should be worth the attention of any business owner who strives to have a high performing company.

Everything is on the table. There's nothing hidden and no more guesswork.

Now, it is simply a matter of choice to embrace this system, or not.

Of course there is work to be done. There is much to relearn, much to learn and much to practice. And, there are proven, effective ways to reach the potential goal (Kanketa SILO Marketing). This brings us to the next Chapter: The SCORECARD

As they say in Japan....

TOKI YOKI!

(High Speed Learning)

CHAPTER 9:

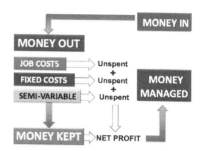

MANAGE WITH A SCORECARD

"What balance should I keep in my business checking account?"
"What should I have for a line of credit?"

And other assorted questions that can be easily answered.

It's great that you are making a profit in your business. Hats off to you. So, exactly what do you keep of what you've earned and what do you do with it?

You keep what you don't spend after you have paid all your expenses.

"Duh, OK, so what's new?" you ask.

The first thing to understand is what you are earning in the first place.

A Kanketa financial Scorecard is a crucial tool for use at any point of business development, from startup, to recovery, to growth and exit.

If you are working in your business, you will have concise information about your business at your fingertips at all times on one 8 ½ piece of paper without a computer, and you'll never lose a dime.

The Scorecard can be used by anyone at any level of the organization. The Scorecard is a very easy to use and it will give you every answer you need to make day to day strategic decisions about paying suppliers, hiring employees, reinvesting, saving, paying Taxes, and best of all, it will show you exactly what you as an owner can pay yourself as each month moves forward without damaging the company.

TOKI YOKI

Before we begin to dig into the details of the Scorecard, I'd like to share with you the most important trip I ever took in my life. It was in 1984. I was on a short flight leaving in a private jet with an executive from a car company.

We were heading up the coast to San Francisco from Irvine California. Twenty minutes after we were airborne from the John Wayne Airport, Mr. Yoshida and I were having a friendly conversation when he was interrupted by a satellite call from his office. I didn't hear all his conversation, but I could tell that it wasn't as pleasant as ours. He was quiet and short with his words. Then he said something that changed my life. He asked a question to the party. "Can I trust you?" Following a brief pause, I heard "Can I trust what you say?"

Then, he pulled out an 8½-by-11 piece of paper from his coat pocket. It was a little tattered and it was clear that he had used this paper a few times before.

"Yes," he said. "Draw up the papers for thirty million." After a few concluding comments, he hung up the phone as though it was just an interruption to his day.

I looked at him in complete surprise. "Excuse me Mr. Yoshida, but did you just happen to sell a company?"

He smiled and acknowledged that he did. I was floored. In the United States we would need a year, a raft of high-paid attorneys and consultants doing due diligence, and a whole army of planners to do what he did in twenty minutes. I begged to understand how he could do such a thing.

"Toki Yoki," he said. "I used my Scorecard." (I later came to understand that "Toki Yoki" is an expression for high-speed learning).

I pleaded with him to share his Scorecard with me, and he did.

Now, remember that in 1984, there were no portable laptop computers to pull out. The IBM Selectric typewriter was considered high-tech. But what he showed me went well beyond computers. His Scorecard contained everything necessary to make any kind of financial decision without ever losing a dime. Two sides of one 8 ½ X 11 piece of paper.

We already know that the Kanketa Normal Balanced Budget is the most important tool in the Kanketa financial management system. Here, we'll look at Mr. Yoshida's piece of paper as we explore the second most important financial element ...

The SCORECARD!

THE SCORECARD LAYOUT

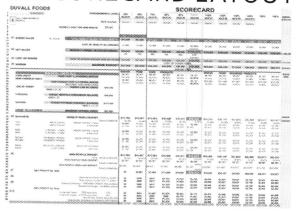

Here you see the Kanketa Scorecard. It looks complicated at first, but when you understand that it contains everything you'll ever need to know about managing your money, you'll realize it's a very friendly document. Planted on a single 8½-by11 piece of paper are all the answers to your money questions. If you allow a little patience, I promise that it will be easy to read, easy to understand, and easy to use.

Perhaps, a Monarch butterfly can tell the Scorecard story best.

Struggling from its cocoon, a beautiful butterfly unfolds. The butterfly will live 30 days. The condition of cocoon from the previous month determines the life of the butterfly in the new month

The butterfly is in complete control with its perfectly centered, balanced body. Its antennas are on constant alert for opportunities.

The parts of its main control center work together continuously to protect, maintain and grow its system in balance.

Its digestive system processes its food, pushing the nutrients forward, while the perfectly weighted abdomen efficiently stores the nourishment and distributes it evenly to the far corners of its wings on demand: forewing at the top, the hindwing at the bottom.

The span of the butterfly's wings extends equally to the left and right. If the left or right wing does not function properly, the butterfly is grounded.

Scorecard Left and Right

Like the butterfly, the out of Balanced Budget pushes its revenue, expenses and profit through the tightly woven cocoon. Once in balance, it unfolds its wings into a beautifully symmetrical Scorecard. The wings are in perfect balance with each other and the budget is now ready to fly.

Each performance column on the Scorecard lives 30 days at a time. The business performance in the previous month determines the budget column of the Scorecard in the new month. Excessive lift on the left wing causes the budget to fly downward. The lift on the right sends the budget upward. The movement must be graceful. If the turn is too quick, the budget is out of control.

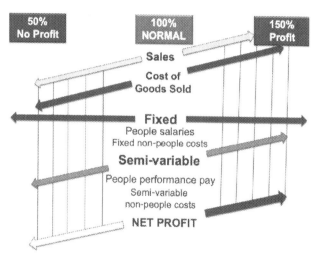

FIG. 9.1

The Scorecard's perfectly balanced body is the 100% Normal center of your company's financial universe. Its marketing antennas are on constant alert for new opportunities.

Your managers are the main control center who work diligently and in unison to continuously protect, maintain and grow your money system.

The evenly balanced Fixed and Semi-Variable expenses help your budget to digest and process its financial nutrients.

The Net Profit is efficiently stored and distributed to the far corners of the wings to provide nourishment.

Let's begin with an overview.

DON'T TRY TO READ OR MAKE SENSE OF THESE NUMBERS.
SEE THE BUTTERFLY SHAPE. GET THE OVERVIEW.

NORMAL
SCORECARD

The Scorecard has a top and bottom section. For our purposes here, we will start with the left wing of the Scorecard and move to the right. Print the left side top on one side of your piece of paper. The left side bottom is on the reverse side. Easy Peasy.

A PERFECT TEN IN BALANCE

The Scorecard displays a 12-month business performance at a glance. The Normal budget is reviewed and updated one time in the first days of each new year. Normal is revised each year based on what occurred in the previous year. No matter what happens in your business for 12 months, the Scorecard remains unchanged.

"But, but, but, my business is so different this year! Our contracts are bigger. Our market is different." Exactly! That is why you do not want to change your Scorecard during the year. When the season becomes more windy or wetter, the butterfly adjusts. The Scorecard will help you stay in balance and battle the changing elements around you.

Performance columns

Across the top, I have numbered each column for your convenience.

Rows

Down the left side of the page, I have renumbered the spreadsheet rows to reflect my own line numbers. This makes it easier to find items and there will be absolutely no confusion about where we are.

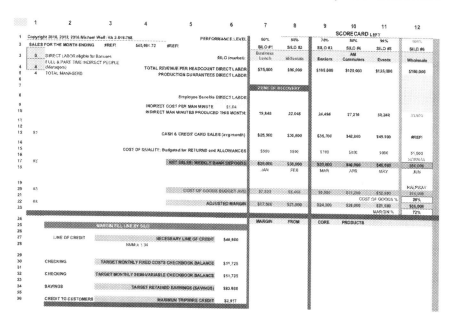

The Scorecard has a wingspan of 11 equal and inseparable parts. Five columns to the left, Normal in the center and five columns to the right.

The sales performance of the previous month will use that performance column as the new month's budget.

The 100% Normal column in the center is your average column from which all other columns are calculated.

Normal is your perfectly Balanced Budget that keeps your company safe and healthy. Normal is the center of your financial universe. If you get this far, you have a good overall understanding of the Scorecard and you are 90% of the way there. Well, ok... maybe 85%

Since the Scorecard only changes once a year, the rest are understanding the details.

DON'T SWEAT THE DETAILS! There are a bunch of refinements and details in the Scorecard that will make your business better, but you'll learn more of the Scorecard by doing, than studying.

The ten critical numbers that you need to know and constantly monitor are all in the Scorecard.

#1.   **Gross Sales** in Kanketa is the money deposited into the depository account from the sale of products and services. We don't count any deposits that are not from products sold.

Cost of Quality is the money that is not charged to a customer: Free samples, rebates, coupons, discounts, returns and rework. The IRS calls these Returns and Allowances

The Cost of Quality budget in the Scorecard increases and decreases in proportion to the Gross Sales. Before you can work with your budget, you must first deduct your Cost of Quality.

Net Sales is the money that is left after removing Cost of Quality, that your company works with to produce products and services. **Last month's Net Sales are used for the current month's budget.**

#2.   **Cost of Goods Sold** tis the money that it costs to produce a job. Cost of Goods Sold are all expenses that are paid OUTSIDE of the company's overhead, including your direct, contracted labor to do the job.

#3.   **Margin** is the operating the money that it costs every month to keep your doors open whether you have $1 or $1 million dollars of business. This is called operating overhead. Margin pays the Fixed expenses, Semi-Variable Costs, and Net Profit.

#4. **One-third of Normal is Fixed cost.** Fixed Costs do not change from month to month, whether sales are at Normal, 50% of Normal, or 150% of Normal. There are two types of Fixed Costs: People (managers) and Non-People (operating costs).

The goal is to keep these Fixed Costs and Semi-Variable Costs in balance with each other.

#5. **Semi-Variable Costs by sales performance column.** Semi-Variable Costs **do** change from month to month in proportion to the performance of the business.

Very Important: Only at Normal do the total of People Fixed Costs plus Non-People Fixed cost (spent and unspent) equal the total of People Semi-Variable Costs plus Non-People Semi-Variable Costs. The100% Normal performance column is the only place on the Scorecard that this balance occurs.

#6. **One-third Net Profit only occurs at Normal.** Net Profit in all other performance columns is calculated by subtracting the total Fixed budget and the total Semi-Variable budget from the Margin in each column. Another way to calculate Net Profit is to subtract the total of People Costs (Fixed and Semi-Variable) and the total of Non-People Costs (Fixed and Semi-Variable) from the Margin. They are the same numbers.

The job of the managers of the operating company (your business as you know it) is to work with the first six numbers on the Scorecard to bring the most Net Profit to the business owner. Your job of keeping the company growing stops here.

The job of the owner is to work with the next four numbers on the Scorecard to keep the company safe by optimizing the Net Profit that the managers produce.

Net Profit has four equal parts in each performance column: reinvestment, Retained Earnings, corporate Taxes and Shareholder Distributions.

#7.   25% Reinvestment

> 12.5% of Net Profit is short-term reinvestment, repaid in 12 months or less
>
> 12.5% of Net Profit is long-term reinvestment, repaid in 13 months or more

#8.   25% Retained Earnings

> 12.5% of Net Profit is short-term Retained Earnings to cover late customer payments, bad debts, and your late bills to your creditors. If you have none of these, your Retained Earnings should go toward your monthly savings.
>
> 12.5% of Net Profit is long-term Retained Earnings in the event of an unforeseen circumstance an unexpected competitor move, market shift, interruptive hazard, etc. If you have none of these, your Retained Earnings should go toward your monthly savings.

#9.   25% Taxes

> Save 17% of Net Profit for year-end corporate Taxes
>
> Save 8% of Net Profit for year-end corporate Taxes

#10.   25% SHAREHOLDER NET INCOME

10 Numbers. The Key Components

Those 10 key numbers on the left side of the Scorecard are the performance components that I just presented.

The Scorecard Wingspan

In row one, you see six columns, with performance levels ranging from 50% to 100%. These are the performance percentages of sales, expenses and profit. This Scorecard continues to the right side of Normal from 100% up to 150%. For now, we will stop at 100% Normal sales performance level.

Column 12 is Normal

Column 12 is your Balanced Budget with all 10 components at 100% Normal that we created in the previous chapter, Set Up Your Budget. Remember that this year's Normal monthly Balanced Budget is derived from last year's Gross Sales divided by 12 months to get this year's monthly budget. All 10 budget expenses are adjusted accordingly.

As you look closely at the 100% Normal column you will see five primary lines of information.

1. Line 13: Cash and credit card sales
2. Line 15: Cost of Quality
3. Line 17: Net Sales (total of weekly bank deposits)
4. Line 20: Cost of Goods budget
5. Line 22: Adjusted Margin

The section between the two red vertical bars is the "Zone of Recovery."

The most important component to your company's profitability is your Margin.

Margin is everything below line 22. The reference area between line 25 and line 36 includes:

- What you need for a line of credit every month to make this all work.
- What you need to keep as your Fixed and Semi-Variable checkbook balances.
- What you should maintain as a savings goal.
- Your "tripwire" credit limit that we will discuss in detail in Chapter 10 is the total credit that you can afford to give to all your customers combined.

SCORECARD LEFT: BOTTOM SECTION

PERFORMANCE PERCENT OF NORMAL

					50%	60%	70%	80%	90%
37	88		MANAGERS:		$1,312.50	$1,406.00	$1,487.50	$1,575.00	$1,662.50	$1,750.00
38									HOURLY	$10.12
39										
40										
41			INDIRECT PEOPLE (MANAGERS)		$5,250	$5,600	$5,950	$6,300	$6,650	$7,000
42			Percent of MARGIN		50.00%	44.44%	40.48%	37.50%	35.19%	33.33%
43	MAKE	Jamie Ruffin DE/MGT PRODN	BACK OFFICE 2 fixed Paid on the 15th		$875	$875	$875	$875	$875	$875
44		Stephanie Ruffin OO/MGT PRODN	2 semi-vari Paid on the 30th		$438	$525	$613	$700	$788	$875
45										
46	SELL	Jamie Ruffin MKTG SALES	FRONT OFFICE 4 fixed Paid on the 15th		$875	$875	$875	$875	$875	$875
47		Stephanie Ruffin MKTG SALES	4 semi-vari Paid on the 30th		$438	$525	$613	$700	$788	$875
48										
49	DELIVER	Tonia Ruffin OC/TY LDRSHP	BACK OFFICE 1 fixed Paid on the 15th		$875	$875	$875	$875	$875	$875
50		Tonia Ruffin CUST CARE	1 semi-vari Paid on the 30th		$438	$525	$613	$700	$788	$875
51										
52	SERVICE	Nina LISTSRV - CARE	BACK OFFICE fixed Paid on the 15th		$875	$875	$875	$875	$875	$875
53		Nina LISTSRV - CARE	semi-vari Paid on the 30th		$438	$525	$613	$700	$788	$875
54										
57		STAFF	Administrative Support:		#REF!	#REF!	#REF!	#REF!	#REF!	#REF!
55			Average Monthly Pay		#REF!	#REF!	#REF!	#REF!	#REF!	#REF!
56			TOTAL Work Hrs Available Per Month		87	104	121	138	156	173
57			TOTAL GROWTH (SEMI-VARIABLE) Hrs Available Per Month		43	52	61	69	78	87
58										
57										
59										
60	88		NON-PEOPLE BUDGET		$5,250	$5,600	$5,950	$6,300	$6,650	$7,000
61			Percent of MARGIN		50.00%	44.44%	40.48%	37.50%	35.19%	33.33%
62			NON-PEOPLE FIXED BUDGET		$3,500	$3,500	$3,500	$3,500	$3,500	$3,500
63			Percent of MARGIN							16.67%
64			NON-PEOPLE SEMI-VARI BUDGET		$1,750	$2,100	$2,450	$2,800	$3,150	$3,500
65										
66						50.00%	44.44%	40.48%	37.50%	35.19%	16.67%
67			Percent of MARGIN							
68	87		NET PROFIT @ Standard Performance		$0	$1,400	$2,800	$4,200	$5,600	$7,000
69			NET PROFIT from UNSPENT overhead		#REF!	#REF!	#REF!	#REF!	#REF!	#REF!
70	88	NET PROFIT for later	REINVESTMENT Short Term repayment 12 months or less		$0	$175	$350	$525	$700	$875
71			REINVESTMENT Long Term repayment 13 months or more		$0	$175	$350	$525	$700	$875
72	88	Busn	RETAINED EARNINGS - (Tripwire Credit for Receivables)		$0	$175	$350	$525	$700	$875
73		Retire	SAVINGS (Safety)		$0	$175	$350	$525	$700	$875
74	810		NET PROFIT for Now (LEASE VALUE)							$3,501
75		TAXES (Corporate) - FED (avg only) 17%		$0	$238	$476	$714	$952	$1,190
76		STATE (avg only) 8%		$0	$112	$224	$336	$448	$560
77		SHAREHOLDERS Distribution Monthly		$0	$175	$350	$525	$700	$875
78		Additional Distributions (Quarterly OPTIONAL)		$0	$175	$350	$525	$700	$875

As you already know, the Normal Monthly Margin in column 12 is the equal balance of one-third People Costs (manager salaries), one-third Non-People (operating overhead) Costs, and one-third Net Profit.

You can see how the Net Profit is divided into the four equal parts:

¼ Reinvestment, ¼ Retained Earnings, 1/4th Taxes, and ¼ th going to Shareholders.

You can see in the Scorecard left that your Normal monthly Balanced Budget has unfolded. The Gross Sales to the left of the 100% Normal column declines in 10 percent increments to 50% of Normal on the low end, and graduates in 10 percent increments to 100% (column 12) on the high end.

Primary information at the bottom of the Scorecard

There are five primary budget lines in the bottom Net Profit section.

1. Line 1-15:   Manager compensation budget, Fixed and Semi-Variable
2. Line 20:   Non-People budget, Fixed and Semi-Variable
3. Line 28:   Net Profit budget
4. Line 29-35:   Net Profit for later – Reinvestment, Retained Earnings
5. Line 37-39:   Taxes

… and the rest (final 1/4th of Net Profit) for Shareholder Distribution

UNFOLD YOUR RIGHT WING

From Normal, the Scorecard extends five columns to the right, out to 150%, again in 10% increments, for a total of 11 Scorecard columns in all (50% to 100% to 150%).

Since most businesses start by performing on the left side of Normal, we will begin on the left.

Normal is Your Minimum Monthly Sales Target

The Scorecard will be the range of your sales performance, the 12 month "sandbox" that you will play in for one year at a time. Here's the good news. As long as you are anywhere in the sandbox, you are always making a profit and your business is safe, healthy and building value.

Certainly you will want your business to perform as far to the right as possible. The objective is to perform slowly, predictably and gracefully with no abruptness.

ACTIVE AND PASSIVE SCORECARDS

Two Scorecards: Active and Passive

There are some simple rules for using the Scorecard to keep your company on track, even when you are absent. If you own a company, you will have to work four hours a week to actively maintain it. When you sell your business, there is no further need to be concerned with Scorecard performance numbers. But, for now, you own it, and your Scorecard is critical to your success with the Kanketa method.

The **Active Scorecard** is used by the Business Leader to manage the day-to-day, and month-to-month operation of the business.

The **Passive Scorecard** is more useful to an absentee owner who is not as concerned with how the company is generally operating.

The passive Scorecard doesn't display the key values built needed for day-to-day management that point at immediate operational concerns. It allows the owner to monitor the general safety and health of the company.

THE BALANCED BUDGET AT THE CENTER
A REVIEW OF NORMAL

"How much should my business expenses be every month if I am in balance"

#1.   GROSS SALES
minus Cost of Quality
NET SALES

#2.   COST OF GOODS SOLD

#3.   MARGIN

#4.   One-third FIXED COSTS
50% People Fixed
50% Non-People Fixed (spent and unspent)

#5.   One-third SEMI-VARIABLE COSTS
50% People Semi-Variable
50% Non-People Semi-Variable (spent and unspent)

#6.   One-third NET PROFIT

#7.   25% of Net Profit - REINVESTMENT
12.5% short-term reinvestment – repaid in 12 months or less
12.5% long-term reinvestment – repaid in 13 months or more

#8.   25% of Net Profit - RETAINED EARNINGS
12.5% short-term Retained Earnings – savings (late customers, payments, bad debts, your late bills to creditors, etc.)
12.5% long-term Retained Earnings – savings in the event of unforeseen circumstances (unexpected competitor move, market shift, interruptive hazard, etc.)

#9.   25% of Net Profit - TAXES
17% Federal – saved for corporate Tax
8% State – saved corporate Tax

#10.   25% of Net Profit - SHAREHOLDER DISTRIBUTION

Every business problem that exists, or has ever existed
is the result of one area of a company
out of balance with another.

All solutions can be found by
putting the company into balance with itself.

Balance internally, and the external forces will follow.
Balance the company, and you will solve the problem.

Mike Wolf

Patience.

　　　　Diligence.

　　　　　　　　Take Your Time.

　　　　　　　　　　　　Understand.

Read. Re-Read. Practice. Practice. Practice.
There are big rewards in your future.

CHAPTER 10:

EXPLORING THE SCORECARD TOP TO BOTTOM

Tracking Your Performance Line By Line

#1 Gross Sales

#2 Cost of Quality, Net Sales

#3 Cost of Goods Sold

#4 Margin

#5 People Costs, Fixed and Semi-Variable

#6 Non-People Costs, Fixed and Semi-Variable

#7 Net Profit for Reinvestment

#8 Retained Earnings

#9 Taxes

#10 Shareholder Distribution

A SCORECARD EXAMPLE: TEN BUDGET ITEMS

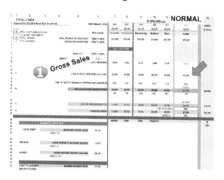

Gross Sales performance is measured by bank deposits. Your last month's cash in the bank establishes the starting point for the new month. Last month's Net Sales determine this month's budget.

As I have said, the Scorecard is a snapshot of your annual budget. Once your budget is set, the 10 budget components need only be revised one time each year. Once Net Sales at Normal and Cost of Goods Sold are established, everything else is a formula that is derived from these two numbers.

At the end of every month, the performance column for the month's GROSS SALES row helps to quickly establish the <u>starting point</u> of next month's budget. But Gross Sales are not the determining factor.

Print your Scorecard on both sides of one piece of 8½-by-11-inch paper for easy viewing. You have a choice here. You can do this by printing the left wing on one side and right wing on the other. You might also consider the top of the Scorecard on one side and the bottom on the other.

The Scorecard alone will answer most of the 30 money management questions in less than 30 seconds, without a computer, without accountants, and without calculators.

If you can't get immediate answers to your 30 questions with just a quick look, you should revisit your budgeting process.

Gross Sales in "Silo Markets" (all columns, line 3)

Kanketa Silos are more specifically defined than markets. Silo Marketing is a separate book. For now, referring to targeted markets is sufficient.

In most small businesses, there is one primary market that makes up 50% of the company's sales. This is typically the market that the business focused on and served best and most often when it opened its doors. The performance of the primary market will typically sustain at least 50% of the Gross Sales since this was the market that the business was founded on.

In Kanketa, it is recommended that the minimum number of target markets that every business should have is six. In our Scorecard, the six markets are identified on line three – one in each performance column. If market #1 keeps the company at 50% of Normal, then each of the five additional markets should add another 10% of Normal to the total sales picture. Ten percent of gross deposits is the minimum sales goal for each of the markets in the performance columns.

Scorecard Percent of Normal Creates Your Safety.

Example: Suppose that last month's total Gross Sales bank deposits from all markets closed at **$43,112**. Our $43,112 amount is in the 90% Gross Sales column our Scorecard example.

10	11	12
80%	90%	100%
SILO #4	SILO #5	SILO #6
Healthcare	Banks	Schools
$108,000	$121,500	$135,000
27,216	30,240	33,600
$36,640	$41,220	$45,800
$640	$720	$800
		NORMAL
$36,000	$40,500	$45,000
APR	MAY	JUN

At first glance our Net Sales is $40,500

The natural tendency is to say that our performance last month was 90% and use column 11 as our new month's budget. However, a closer glance at this same example might tell us differently.

Accurate Accounting Is Critical.

Suppose that **Net Sales,** after removing Cost of Quality, was actually $39,418 according to our accounting records. Net Sales would be in the 80% column. Because Net Sales did not quite hit the $40,500 mark of 90%, we must use the 80% performance column for our current month's budget, which is $36,000 Net Sales in column 10.

How does this help you, the owner?

	50%	60%	70%	80%	90%	100%
NET PROFIT @ Standard Performance	$0	$1,400	$2,800	$4,200	$5,600	$7,000

You, (hopefully traveling to some exotic place on a six month vacation with your family or friends), know from a quick glance at the corresponding Net Profit in column 10 on your Scorecard that you have a reliable profit disbursement from your company based on last month's 80% performance level. You can confidently instruct your office to deposit $4,200 into your personal bank account without questioning the amount.

This is your Scorecard performance profit that you can safely take from the business without damaging it IF you have good control of Cost of Quality. If Cost of Quality is significant, your owner's profit could be off a bit. The good news is that it won't be enough to do a lot of damage before you return.

It is not the total profit that you made for the month. Your owner's expenses are in that profit. You still must pay any Reinvestment, deposit into Savings, and save for Corporate Taxes.

Your Business Leader back at the ranch must manage all expenses in order to make this happen. In this case, the company may not exceed the expense budget of 80% including the Cost of Goods Sold (column 10, line 20) as well as the 80% Margin with expenses of $28,000 (column 10, line 22).

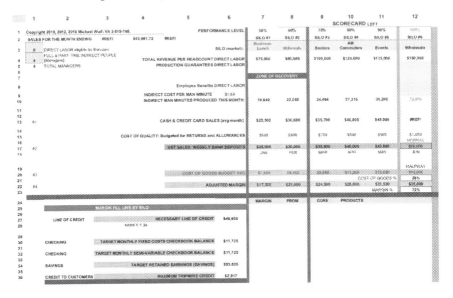

Your Business Leader who is managing your company, is not responsible for anything below the Net Profit line. They are hired for one purpose only: to deliver the Net Profit.

It will be you, the owner, who will decide to reinvest into your business.
It will be you, the owner, who will decide when and how much debts to pay.
It will be you, the owner, who will decide to put money into your savings account.
It will be you, the owner, who will decide to pay your corporate tax or put taxes into your tax account.

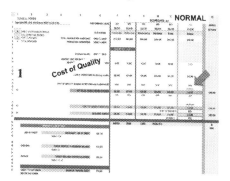

Before settling on the month's Gross Sales number as our budget, we must first identify and subtract all Cost of Quality from the deposits. This covers any non-recoverable costs such as free samples, returns, rework, warranties, and cost of error for the month.

	50%	60%	70%	**80%**	90%
COST OF QUALITY: Budgeted for RETURNS and ALLOWANCES	$400	$480	$560	$640	$720
NET SALES: WEEKLY BANK DEPOSITS	$22,500	$27,000	$31,500	$36,000	$40,500
	JAN	FEB	MAR	APR	MAY

If Cost of Quality is not recognized as actual non-recoverable expenses and subtracted from Gross Sales, they will automatically be paid later from the owner's Net Profit.

In this example, last month's Net Sales closed out at $39,418.00 (in the 80% of Normal performance column). In this case we would subtract the $640 budgeted for Cost of Quality (for free giveaways, free samples, cost of returned items, cost of rework, etc.) to get $38,778 in Net Sales for last month. This Net Sales amount becomes the current month's budget.

NET SALES TO THE RIGHT SIDE OF NORMAL

			NORMAL											
4	5	6	12	U	V	W	X	Y	Z	AA	AB	AC	AD	AE	13
	PERFORMANCE LEVEL		100%	110%		120%		130%		140%		150%		150%	ANNUAL
$43,798.20	96%		SLO #6	SLO #7		SLO #8		SLO #9		SLO #10					% Normal
	S&O (market):		Schools	SLO #7		SLO #8		SLO #9		SLO #12		BUCKET			
ANNUAL REVENUE PER MGR. HEADCOUNT	DIRECT LABOR		$135,000	$148,500		$162,000		$175,500		$189,000		$202,500			
PRODUCTION GUARANTEES	DIRECT LABOR														
Employee Benefits	DIRECT LABOR														
INDIRECT COST PER MAN MINUTE	$0.83														
INDIRECT MAN MINUTES PRODUCED THIS MONTH			33,636	36,366		44,382		57,858		90,723		121,081		181,621	$403,206
CASH & CREDIT CARD SALES (avg month)			$45,500	$50,380		$54,300		$59,840		$63,550		$57,375		$57,375	$549,006
COST OF QUALITY: Budgeted for RETURNS and ALLOWANCES			$830	$896		$962		$1,048		$1,136		$1,208		$1,208	$6,806
			NORMAL												
NET SALES WEEKLY BANK DEPOSITS			$45,500	$49,500		$54,000		$58,500		$63,000		$67,500		$67,500	$540,006
			JUN	JUL		AUG		SEP		OCT		NOV		DEC	
			HALFWAY												
COST OF GOODS BUDGET AVG			$24,000	$26,400		$28,800		$31,200		$33,600		$36,000		$36,000	$288,000
			53%	53%											
ADJUSTED MARGIN			$21,000	$23,100		$25,410		$27,931		$30,746		$33,821		$33,821	$252,000
			47%												

While the same rules apply on the right side of Normal, the considerations for the budget increase will change.

Since the business has advanced beyond 100% Normal performance, there is an incremental money surplus on all lines throughout (except in Fixed Costs which do not change at any performance level).

The goal on the right side of Normal is to keep all costs as close to Normal levels as possible. The more that is unspent, the more money in each category falls to the owner's bottom line.

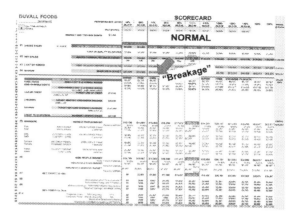

Let's talk for a moment about the HIDDEN money in your business. The Kanketa system considers every penny. Nothing falls through the cracks. This is how Mr. Yoshida could consider selling off a $30,000,000 company in 20 minutes. He knew that he would not lose on the deal no matter how grim it might have sounded - because of his "Breakage."

When was the last time you recall any company achieving an exact even Net Sales number to the penny in a performance column? $60,000? $70,000? $80,000? The likelihood is in the million-to-one range. The point here is that your Net Sales number for the month will always will fall between two performance columns. The money in between any two **Net Sales** columns is called Breakage.

Breakage is the month's actual Net Sales of products and services (after Cost of Quality) minus the budgeted Net Sales in the performance column minus Cost of Goods Sold. This is your Breakage.

Example: The actual Net Sales (after Cost of Quality) is $74,428 (more than $70,000, but less than the $80,000 performance level) minus the budgeted Net Sales of the performance column itself ($70,000) = $4,428 Breakage minus Cost of Goods Sold (example $1,100) = $3,328, Breakage.

Since the business operates in hard cutoffs of 70% of Normal, 80% of Normal, 90% of Normal and so on, the Breakage Margin (after Cost of Goods Sold) will fall to the bottom line.

BREAKAGE STARTS AT NET SALES

Cost of Quality is in and out money. Cost of Quality is not kept by the business to pay operating expenses. In all cases, the Net Sale is the amount of money that the company keeps and can confidently count on and work with.

Let's say that in another example below, last month's bank deposits closed out at $216,527.00. Since deposits didn't hit $240,000 (80% of Normal) we will stay in the 70% performance column of $210,000. Suppose that mixed in with the deposits are some other income of $1,216 not related to our products and services. We will subtract unrelated income, leaving deposits of $215,331.33 Next, we will subtract any Cost of Quality (example: $1,949.27 total discounts given to customers) to get to Net Sales for the previous month of $213,382.06. The we will subtract the net sale budget of $210,000 in the 70% performance column from the actual Net Sales deposited. Our Breakage is now $3,382.06. Finally we will subtract Cost of Goods from our Breakage.

For all you number lovers: In our example, the $69,668 Margin budget in the 70% column divided by $140,332 = 49.6% of Net Sales is the Margin percentage after Cost of Goods Sold. Our Breakage of $3,382.06 X 49.6% = $1,677.50 extra profit for the owner.

For all you number haters: Anyone in business must know their general Cost of Goods Sold percent of sales on their P&L. Use that percent.

	50%	60%	70%	80%
NEW 1st X OPPORTUNITIES	$127,500	$153,000	$178,500	$204,000
NET SALES CLOSED	$150,000	$180,000	$210,000	$240,000
COST OF GOODS BUDGET	$100,237	$120,285	$140,332	$160,379
MARGIN	$49,763	$59,715	$69,668	$79,621

At the end of each month, Breakage is sitting untouched in your main company checking account, ready to pay to the Owner-Shareholders. The monthly Breakage possibility is between 1% and 9% of the Margin. This can be quite significant over the year since it almost always happens every month.

COST OF GOODS SOLD
Budget Item #3 of 10

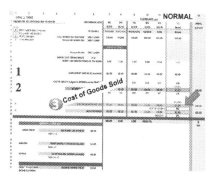

The next item on our Scorecard is Cost of Goods Sold. In addition to the Cost of Quality, we must subtract the Cost of Goods Sold budget amount before we can spend the Margin. Cost of Goods Sold is the amount of money that is costs to produce all products and services for the month. In our Scorecard, the Cost of Goods Sold at 80% of Normal is $19,200.

Performance:	50%	60%	70%	80%	90%
COST OF GOODS BUDGET AVG	$12,000	$14,400	$16,800	$19,200	$21,600
					COST OF GOODS %
ADJUSTED MARGIN	$10,500	$12,600	$14,700	$16,800	$18,900
					MARGIN %

Important: Cost of Goods Sold is strictly determined from the items that show up in your bank statements. Do not pay cash for Cost of Goods Sold expenses unless there is a specifically identified fund designated for this purpose, with receipts for each expense. Random unidentified cash transactions without receipts are not part of this system.

12	13	14	15	16	17
100%	110%	120%	130%	140%	150%

NORMAL						
$45,000	$49,500	$54,000	$58,500	$63,000	$67,500	$67,500
JUN	JUL	AUG	SEP	OCT	NOV	DEC
HALFWAY						
$24,000	$26,400	$28,800	$31,200	$33,600	$36,000	$36,000
53%	53%					
$21,000	$23,100	$25,410	$27,951	$30,746	$33,821	$33,821
47%						

Cost of Goods Sold that run parallel to Gross Sales should increase and decrease proportionately with the amount of work. In my experience, the companies that consistently perform on the right side of Normal are less focused on problems and more focused on growth. They seem to become more aware of and more efficient in the control of job costs as they apply the Kanketa principles.

With better management of vendors, the opportunity to save money in each of the budget categories creates a contribution to Net Profit.

You should not count an automatic contribution to profit from unspent Cost of Goods Sold, but you should always count on the opportunity to create more profit on the right side from unspent budgets.

What's with those months under each performance column?

I put the months in each performance column as a point of reference for marketing planning purposes. By January, you should be reasonably certain that at least 50% of Normal will be achieved for the year. By February you should be able to identify another 10% of your Normal sales target. If all goes well, by June, you should be at Normal and on your way to 150% of Normal.

It's just a gauge against your annual sales objective, but you might find it helpful.

Margin, margin, margin. It's all about margin!

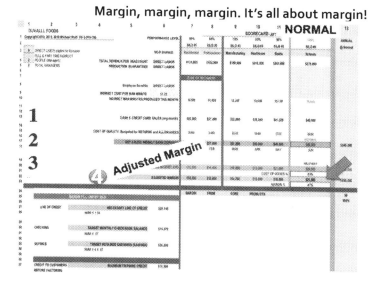

There are some business owners who lose so much money from low Margins, they won't even read a book with Margins in it.

Your Margin is the Most Important Number in Your Business.

After Net Sales are determined, and Cost of Goods Sold are removed, all remaining expenses for the month are in the Margin. As you have seen, Margin is the only place where your company grows. In your Margin, you will win or lose. It is Margin that will determine the value at sale or lease of your company. Margin in balance is the goal for a safe, high performing company.

Why "Adjusted"?

A Margin budget is approximate. Round numbers are easier to remember and easier to work with. An adjustment up or down to the nearest $5,000 sound like a lot, but "to the nearest" means an adjustment of up to half of the difference.

It's an acceptable variation for $2,500 to be dispersed between all Margin costs because the differences between incremental budget costs in the performance columns are small.

If Semi-Variable Costs alone had eight items that would be part of this adjustment, the budget differences would be manageable. Remember, it's a budget, not actual.

Your business should develop marketing and sales processes for achieving the adjusted Margin if your adjustment is an increase.

If your Margin is $36,000, adjust to $35,000. You may be conservative or aggressive, but just remember that your adjustment will affect your wages, your Fixed Costs, your Semi-Variable Costs, and the Net Profit balance.

OTHER SCORECARD DITTIES

3	0	DIRECT LABOR eligible for Bonuses
4	4	FULL & PART TIME INDIRECT PEOPLE (Managers)
5	4	TOTAL MANAGERS
6		
7		

indirect Man Minutes Sold and Produced Last Month

		50%	60%	70%	80%	90%	100%
INDIRECT COST PER MAN MINUTE	$0.63						
INDIRECT MAN MINUTES PRODUCED THIS MONTH:		19,840	22,045	24,494	27,216	30,240	33,600

Man Minutes (column 6, row 9)

In Kanketa, one of the ways that budgets are controlled is through a measured increment of time called a "man minute." Because man minutes are used in global companies, I do not have the luxury of being more politically correct with the term "person minutes."

A man minute is your number of indirect People time (managers - full time or half time) X 8,400 work minutes per month. Eight-thousand-four-hundred work minutes is a constant and never changes.

Example A: Four managers X 8,400 minutes a month = 25,200-man minutes of time per month available for the company to sell. In our Scorecard there are four managers X 8,400 minutes a month each or 33,600 total man minutes of time per month for sale.

Cost Per Man Minute

To find the cost to the company (dollar value) of one man minute, divide your monthly Margin at Normal by your total man minutes.

	50%	60%	70%	80%	90%
COST OF GOODS BUDGET AVG	$12,000	$14,400	$16,800	$19,200	$21,600
					COST OF GOODS %
ADJUSTED MARGIN	$10,500	$12,600	$14,700	$16,800	$18,900
					MARGIN %

In this example, the monthly Margin at Normal is $18,900, divided by 25,200 man minutes is $.75 per man minute that it is costing the company for every minute of every person worked.

At 80% of Net Sales in the above figure, we have only sold 27,216 man minutes in the previous month. In other words, the company sold 27,216 man minutes at $.75 each for every minute of time that a manager showed up for work ...

... or does work
... or eats lunch
... or goes to the bathroom
... or has meetings
... or talks on their cellphone

Time or Distance: Man Minutes or Clock Feet

It takes an average adult 60 seconds to walk 400 feet. In Kanketa a man minute of time is equivalent to a "clock foot" distance of movement.

Why is this important? Let me ask, how much does it cost you in man minutes to quote a job? Make a product? Package and ship? Do a survey? Fetch Inventory? Make a delivery? This is important to know so that, through the use of man minutes you can very accurately price your services.

Remember that a man minute is 1/60th of the Margin at Normal. If the Margin consists of Fixed and Semi-Variable Costs in balance, People Costs and Non-People Costs in balance and a balanced Net Profit for the owner. Then, there is no reason to calculate Net Profit further. All operational overhead plus Net Profit is included when you use man minutes.

Track Man Minutes, Not Markups.

Markups can be guesswork.

Why would you bother to mark up a product or service when you sell it? Simply add all of the man minutes in time that it takes to complete every step of design, development, production, processing and/or management of any product you sell, to the Cost of Goods Sold and you will have a perfect "markup".

This also means that adding a percent to something you sell can be an absolute guess. You can only equate a markup percentage amount by dividing the markup by your man minute costs to get the amount of minutes of time that you just sold (your human inventory).

What is Your Time Worth?

This brings me to a bigger question. What about you? My answer is: It depends upon who you are at the moment.

If you are a production worker in your company

You are out in the shop or you are working in a Workroom IN your business, you are worth what you can hire someone else to do. You are worth your man minute cost multiplied by 60 (your hourly rate as a worker).

If you are a Workroom manager in your company

As a Workroom manager hired by the Business Leader of the company (who might be you) to manage two Workroom corridors, your Fixed wage per month is 4.17% of Margin at Normal to maintain the Workroom performance, and 4.17% of Margin multiplied by the previous month's performance column percent of Normal to grow your Workroom.

If you are the Business Leader of your company

You might be the Business Leader who is managing your company, hired by the owner (who might be you) to manage the owner's company (which might be yours).

As a Business Leader, your time is worth the man minute cost of one-third of the Margin of a management company of the owner that you might work for.

Half of the Business Leader's Fixed salary is paid for maintaining the performance of the operating company (which right now is your company). The other half of the Business Leader's Performance Compensation is for your ability to grow your company through good leadership.

The Business Leader's man minute cost is the Net Profit of your company at Normal divided by 8,400 minutes a month.

If you are the owner of your company

Then, forget all of this and divide your last year's taxable income by 1,000 to get your hourly value as the owner of your business. Up to 1,000 hours a year is what the owner has available to work ON the business, creating strategies, processes and procedures for the Business Leader to carry out. If you filed Taxes on $85,000 last year, your hourly rate this year is $85 per hour.

If you are a company of one, you are the owner, and the management team of your company.

YOUR SCORECARD "BATTER'S BOX"

(Middle of the scorecard)

	MARGIN FILL LINE BY SILO	
LINE OF CREDIT	NECESSARY LINE OF CREDIT (Margin at Normal X 1.8) NMM X 1.8	$54,000
CHECKING	TARGET MONTHLY FIXED COSTS CHECKBOOK BALANCE	$10,050
CHECKING	TARGET MONTHLY SEMI-VARIABLE CHECKBOOK BALANCE	$10,050
SAVINGS	TARGET RETAINED EARNINGS (SAVINGS)	$80,400
CREDIT TO CUSTOMERS	MAXIMUM TRIPWIRE CREDIT (Net Profit at Normal div. by 8 X 12)	$15,000

NECESSARY LINE OF CREDIT

"What should I have for a line of credit?"

Normal Monthly Margin multiplied by 1.8 is the maximum amount of money needed to operate your company every month if you are managing your money with the Money Map. If you need more than this, you are probably not managing your expenses efficiently.

YOUR BUSINESS CHECKBOOK BALANCE

"What balance should I keep in the business checking account?"

What should your total balance be in all checking accounts that the business maintains? Normal Monthly Margin multiplied by .67 is the ideal total amount of money that should always be in your accounts.

"How much should I have in corporate savings?"

A GOOD MONTHLY TARGET FOR SAVINGS

Normal Monthly Margin X 4 X .67 is the ideal amount of money needed to keep the company safe from unexpected turbulence. This is a target and will take time to build. A minimum of 25% of your Net Profit in the performance column of your Scorecard should be deposited every month into savings. One-half of your Net Profit shouldn't be touched. The other half should be your maximum accounts receivable between 31 and 89 days.

"How much credit should I give to my customers?"

MAXIMUM CREDIT AVAILABLE TO YOUR CUSTOMERS

How much credit should you give to all of your customers combined at any one time? This amount is called tripwire credit.

Fifty percent one month of Normal Monthly Margin is the maximum amount of credit beyond 30 days that a financially safe company can afford to give to all customers combined.

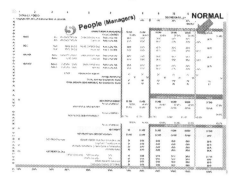

Direct Labor Cost – the folks who are hired for each job at an hourly rate is part of Cost of Goods Sold, not the People Costs shown here.

People Costs are Indirect Managers. These are the employees on your staff who work on many jobs at one time, who must show up every day whether you make $1 or $1 million dollars in sales.

			50%	60%	70%	80%	90%	
		INDIRECT PEOPLE (MANAGERS)	$5,250	$5,888	$5,950	$6,300	$6,650	$7,000
		Percent of MARGIN	50.00%	44.44%	40.48%	37.50%	35.19%	33.33%
MAKE	Richard DuVall OCMGT PRODN	BACK OFFICE 2 fixed Paid on the 15th	$875	$875	$875	$875	$875	$875
	Richard DuVall OCMGT PRODN	2 semi-vari Paid on the 30th	$438	$525	$613	$700	$788	$875
SELL	Karen White MKTG SALES	FRONT OFFICE 4 fixed Paid on the 15th	$875	$875	$875	$875	$875	$875
	Karen White MKTG SALES	4 semi-vari Paid on the 30th	$438	$525	$613	$700	$788	$875
DELIVER	Steve Erickson OCITY LDRSHP	BACK OFFICE 1 fixed Paid on the 15th	$875	$875	$875	$875	$875	$875
	Steve Erickson CUST CARE	1 semi-vari Paid on the 30th	$438	$525	$613	$700	$788	$875
SERVICE	Sandy DuVall USTSRV - CARE	BACK OFFICE fixed Paid on the 15th	$875	$875	$875	$875	$875	$875
	Sandy DuVall USTSRV - CARE	semi-vari Paid on the 30th	$438	$525	$613	$700	$788	$875
	STAFF	Administrative Support:	#REF!	#REF!	#REF!	#REF!	#REF!	#REF!
		Average Monthly Pay	#REF!	#REF!	#REF!	#REF!	#REF!	#REF!
		TOTAL Work Hrs Available Per Month	87	104	121	138	156	173
		TOTAL GROWTH (SEMI-VARIABLE) Hrs Available Per Month	43	52	61	69	78	87

I suggest that pay days are twice per month. I will also suggest that payroll is no later than the 10th and no later than the 25th of the month. A company should close out the previous month by the 10th day of the new month. The goal is to only touch money two hours a month with flawless transactions.

Indirect Manager Compensations

PAY FIXED SALARIES FOR ALL MANAGERS ON A DAY BETWEEN THE 1st AND THE 15th

(by the 10th of the month is suggested).

PAY SEMI-VARIABLE PERFORMANCE FOR ALL MANAGERS ON A DAY BETWEEN THE 16th AND THE LAST DAY OF THE MONTH (by the 25th of the month is suggested).

In our 80% performance column on the Scorecard: Each manager would receive a gross pre-tax Fixed salary paycheck of $875 between the 1st and the 10th.

And a Semi-Variable gross, pre-tax performance paycheck of $700 at 80% performance between the 16th and the 25th of the month.

On row 58, this company decided that Steve Erickson would do the office administration (billing, budget management, etc.) within the scope of his job. There is no added budget for Steve. Individual payroll taxes are paid by the managers.

All 941 company matching of FUTA, SUTA and FICA withholding is separately paid by the company from the Non-People budget. For a quick number I use total W2 payroll X .1765.

Annual Revenue Per Head Count

Revenue per head is unique to each industry type.

I am going to tell you this purely from my own experiences with the 26 companies I have owned in my life. You decide for yourself.

I ran companies of 30 employees with the four House of Value Workroom managers. I personally held the position of Business Leader until I could find one. After 30 employees (between $3 and $6 million dollars in annual sales) I began to put corridor managers in place. I never had more than eight managers for up to $23,500,000 a year in annual sales (two corridor managers per Workroom) or approximately one manager per $3 million in annual sales.

Finish one thing at a time, then start another was our mantra. Each manager had no more than six direct labor workers who reported to them

Hire no more than four managers for up to 30 employees - one for each Workroom - with two areas of responsibilities assigned to each.

The 100% Normal sales performance on the Scorecard times 12 months reflects the minimum annual amount of sales that your managers are collectively responsible to achieve for half of their compensation as a Fixed salary.

RESPONSIBILITIES OF WORKROOM MANAGERS

Marketing   Must maintain Normal sales volume of new, first-time prospect opportunities.

Sales   Must convert marketing opportunities into a percentage of first-time customer payments (contracts sold).

Customer Service

Must ensure that all customers are fully satisfied with every transaction – error free.

Customer Care

Must ensure that 80% of Normal sales volume of first-time customers become continuous, annually repeating opportunities.

Product Management

Must design the product or service profitably, with all purchasing done at a supplier cost that guarantees it.

Production   Must produce the product within budget – error free.

Velocity   Must deliver first-time job volume satisfactorily – on time.

Self-Directed Leadership

Must maintain employee productivity and employee engagement within the allowed People compensation budgets.

PEOPLE COSTS
TO THE RIGHT OF NORMAL

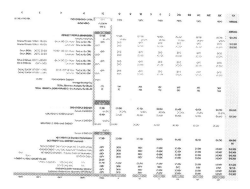

There's an old saying that you can't get people to do want you want. You can only get people to do what you pay them for. I don't think it's as old as they say.

An interesting thing happens to the right of Normal. Attitudes change. Motivations change. Attentions change. Enthusiasms change. When a company starts performing on the right side of Normal, attitudes shift and performance becomes a whole new ballgame. Good management and leadership really need to kick in to keep up the momentum.

I have always lived by the belief that you manage in meetings. In meetings you are collaborating, solving problems, and creating clarity and agreement. When people disband, they return to their stations to carry out what they came away with in the meetings.

To the right of Normal is the budget that follows the result of the team's accomplishment. People are more willing to understand, agree with and see the personal benefit of adhering to budget rules because they are experiencing the positive benefits of this budgeting system. After all, they are earning more money on the right side.

#1	Gross Sales
#2	Cost of Quality, Net Sales
#3	Cost of Goods Sold
#4	Margin
#5	People Costs, Fixed and Semi-Variable
#6	Non-People Costs, Fixed and Semi-Variable
#7	Net Profit for reinvestment
#8	Retained Earnings
#9	Taxes
#10	Shareholder Distribution

MANAGER PAY – ON THE RIGHT SIDE OF NORMAL

INDIRECT PEOPLE (MANAGERS)	$7,000	$7,350	$7,700	$8,050	$8,400	$8,750	$8,750
Percent of MARGIN	33.33%	31.82%	30.30%	28.80%	27.32%	25.87%	25.87%
BACK OFFICE 2 fixed Paid on the 15th	$875	$875	$875	$875	$875	$875	$875
2 semi-vari Paid on the 30th	$875	$963	$1,050	$1,138	$1,225	$1,313	$1,313
FRONT OFFICE 4 fixed Paid on the 15th	$875	$875	$875	$875	$875	$875	$875
4 semi-vari Paid on the 30th	$875	$963	$1,050	$1,138	$1,225	$1,313	$1,313
BACK OFFICE 1 fixed Paid on the 15th	$875	$875	$875	$875	$875	$875	$875
1 semi-vari Paid on the 30th	$875	$963	$1,050	$1,138	$1,225	$1,313	$1,313
BACK OFFICE fixed Paid on the 15th	$875	$875	$875	$875	$875	$875	$875
semi-vari Paid on the 30th	$875	$963	$1,050	$1,138	$1,225	$1,313	$1,313
Administrative Support:	&REF!						

Indirect People Costs (managers) to the right of Normal grow incrementally by ten percent. It is important to hold each manager to their responsibilities to ensure that they are growing the company.

It is not a good idea to allow managers to think that the right side is automatically going to give them a performance bonus that is achieved by the team. A manager might take on the mindset that they can relax, because the team will produce.

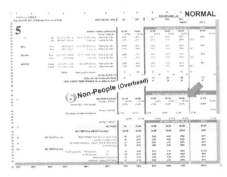

Non-People Costs follow the same balanced contour: Half FIXED and half SEMI-VARIABLE

	50%	60%	70%	80%	90%	NORMAL
			NON-PEOPLE COSTS PAYMENT BUDGET			$7,000
NON-PEOPLE BUDGET	$5,250	$5,600	$5,950	$6,300	$6,650	$7,000
Percent of MARGIN	50.00%	44.44%	40.48%	37.50%	35.19%	33.33%
NON-PEOPLE FIXED BUDGET	$3,500	$3,500	$3,500	$3,500	$3,500	$3,500
Percent of MARGIN						16.67%
NON-PEOPLE SEMI-VARI BUDGET	$1,750	$2,100	$2,450	$2,800	$3,150	$3,500

Fixed Non-People Costs are the amount of money to pay for operating costs that do not change from month to month (by more than 5% in a performance column).

Non-People Fixed Costs would include rent, cellphone contracts, cleaning service contracts, insurance payments, etc. Therefore, in the 80% column, the Fixed cost budget of $3,500 does not change from $3,500 at Normal.

Semi-Variable Non-People Costs are the operating costs that DO change slightly from month to month. In the 80% column, the Semi-Variable cost budget of $2,800 changed from Normal of $3,500 by 20%.

At 80% there are fewer costs for office supplies because the business decreases, and there more costs for office supplies when the business increases.

Fewer costs for gas to service existing customers when the business decreases.
More costs for gas to service existing customers when the business increases.

Fewer costs for utilities when the business decreases.
More costs for utilities when the business increases.

Get the picture?

Non-People Costs are managed at a micro-level by month-to-month comparisons on the accountant's monthly profit and loss statements. However, if the main expense categories are in balance, there is no real urgency to be concerned about detail beyond this. Typically, the individual item details on the accountant's P&L is reviewed quarterly.

If a main expense category exceeds the budget, go to the details to home in on the costs of each item.

Adjust the individual item costs. Don't change the overall Fixed to Semi-Variable balance when you exceed your budget.

Can the cost item such as cellphones, office supplies, waste management, etc., be rethought? Reassigned? Outsourced? Eliminated? Reduced? Redesigned? Get creative. Put your budget back in line as quickly as you can.

CHAPTER 11:

KEEP YOUR NET PROFIT USING YOUR SCORECARD

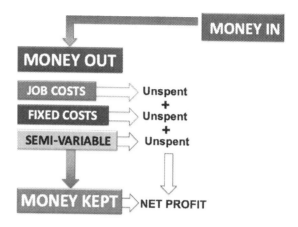

NET PROFIT FOR SHAREHOLDERS

"I've got to pay my people; so I guess just won't take a paycheck this month."

The only reason that an owner might not take a Net Profit check is because the company is out of balance by more than 10% in its Fixed and/or Semi-Variable Costs. Balance the company and you won't be short of money to pay yourself.

Owners are in business to put money into their own pockets. Since the Kanketa system is all about balance, Kanketa places equal value on all four Net Profit responsibilities of the owner: reinvestment, Retained Earnings, Taxes, and owner-Shareholder earnings.

True Story: If you loan it, you own it.

Ethan F.'s transportation company in the Bronx transports seniors who live in assisted living residences. Every month Ethan invoices state-run health care facilities. Every month it's the same story – the State of New York pays late. But, if you want the business, it's something you must accept.

On occasion, Ethan finds himself saying, "I've got to pay my People; so, I guess I just won't take a paycheck this month." This happens at least once a quarter. When I totaled up what Ethan made a year versus what he thinks he made, his earnings are significantly less that he imagined. This is because Ethan has adjusted his lifestyle, and this isn't so much the problem.

Ethan plans to sell his company, which is a C corporation. The new buyers are willing to pay all the legitimate debts as part of the sale. When Ethan didn't pay himself four times his monthly wage a year for the last six years (about 24 times in all), he should have taken his wage from the company, paid Taxes, and on the same day loaned back the after-Tax net amount. Had he done this all along, updating a loan agreement from himself personally to the corporate entity, he would have received $6,000 per month multiplied by 24 months of back wages ($144,000 extra dollars) at the time of sale before the company was purchased at its current net value.

You aren't your company. At incorporation, your operating agreement says that you have declared yourself a salary for working in your company as an employee. If the company cannot pay you what it owes you, you should extract your gross wage payments, deposit them into your personal checkbook, put 25% away for personal Taxes, create and update a loan document, and on the same day loan yourself back your take home compensation to the company, if required. This loan is on your books until it is paid. See your accountant about this, because the approach can be slightly different with each type of company. A Sub-S corporation might attack this differently than if your company is an LLC, a C corporation, and so on.

Note: You may not repay loans due to you as an owner with a bank or SBA loan.

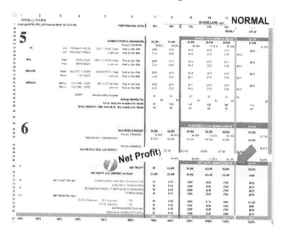

No, you probably can't buy the boat just yet. And, yes, the Net Profit is just another budget item at this point. Business owners are continuously called upon by the company to continue to do their part; to reinvest to remain competitive; save in case of an emergency or unforeseen opportunity; and keep compliant with the government.

Standing back, let's take another look at the full Scorecard.

DUVALL FOODS (example)

SCORECARD

(The scorecard is a large financial spreadsheet with rows labeled lines 1–68, including GROSS SALES, COST OF QUALITY ALLOWANCE, NET SALES, COST OF GOODS, MARGIN, FIXED COSTS, SEMI-VARIABLE COSTS, LINE OF CREDIT, CHECKING, SAVINGS, CREDIT TO CUSTOMERS, MANAGERS, INDIRECT PEOPLE BUDGET, NON-PEOPLE BUDGET, NET PROFIT for later, NET PROFIT for Now, and performance level columns from 50% through 180% and ANNUAL @ Normal. The numeric detail is not legible enough to transcribe reliably.)

Lines 58 through 68 are the eight parts of Net Profit, for later, and for now.

#8:   12.5% Reinvestment Short Term
         12.5% Reinvestment Long Term

#9:   12.5% Retained Earning Short Term
         12.5% Retained Earning Long Term

#10.   17% Corporate Tax - Federal
         8% Corporate Tax - State

12.5% Owner-Shareholder Distribution monthly
12.5% Owner-Shareholder Distribution Quarterly, Bi-annually and/or annually

Beginning with the total Net Profit for the month:

					50%	60%	70%	80%	90%
68	87			NET PROFIT @ Standard Performance	$0	$1,400	$2,800	$4,200	$5,600	$7,000
69				NET PROFIT from UNSPENT overhead	#REF!	#REF!	#REF!	#REF!	#REF!	#REF!
70	88	NET PROFIT for later		REINVESTMENT Short Term repayment 12 months or less	$0	$175	$350	$525	$700	$875
71				REINVESTMENT Long Term repayment 13 months or more	$0	$175	$350	$525	$700	$875
72	89		Busn	RETAINED EARNINGS - (Tapwire Credit for Receivables)	$0	$175	$350	$525	$700	$875
73			Retire	SAVINGS (Safety)	$0	$175	$350	$525	$700	$875
74	810	NET PROFIT for Now (LEASE VALUE)								$3,501
75				TAXES (Corporate) - FED (avg only) 17%	$0	$238	$476	$714	$952	$1,190
76				STATE (avg only) 8%	$0	$112	$224	$336	$448	$560
77				SHAREHOLDERS Distribution Monthly	$0	$175	$350	$525	$700	$875
78				Additional Distributions (Quarterly OPTIONAL)	$0	$175	$350	$525	$700	$875

In the 80% Net Profit column in our example, the owner would have $4,200 left in the bank from the previous month after paying all operating expenses.

Profit for Later: Reinvestment

25% of the $4,200 Net Profit is used for reinvestment into the business (12.5% of Net Profit for short term and 12.5% for long term). Reinvestment is for business growth, <u>not for paying back debt</u>.

One-eighth of Net Profit, or $525 is used for **short-term,** one-time reinvestments into business growth (a one-time cost for a new website, a one-time new hire that won't be productive for a few months, a one-time small piece of equipment that will show a return or be repaid within the current calendar or fiscal year from the day it was paid, etc.)

One-eighth of Net Profit, or $525 from last month, is used for **reinvestment** for **long-term** business growth (a total single principal payment or total of principal payments of an investment that will show a return or be repaid in 13 months or more from the day it was paid, etc.)

Profit for Later: Retained Earnings

One eighth of Net Profit, or $525 from last month is used for **Retained Earnings** - to grow the business savings account in the **long term** in the event of unforeseen and unexpected turbulence or response to a new opportunity.

One-eighth of Net Profit, or $525 from last month, is used for **Retained Earnings short term** – supporting potential debt and for paying back debt or bad debt. Retained Earnings (12.5% of Net Profit) is a budget that shouldn't be spent in the B2B world for accounts payable over 31 days.

This is a safety valve for bad debts and customers who go out of business. After 30 days, customers who haven't paid are borrowing your necessary savings to operate their business, instead of borrowing from a bank.

The farther to the left of Normal you get, the less you have for debt repayment.

Your allowance to pay toward back debts in the current month in Retained Earnings changes in each performance column. The goal is to continue to lower your overall debt so that, ideally, your Retained Earnings money can be routinely put into a business savings account.

One-eighth of this, or $525 from last month, is saved for corporate Taxes. I use a rule of thumb of 17% for federal and 8% for state.

One-fourth of Net Profit, or in our example, $1,050 from last month, is distributed to owner-Shareholders.

NET PROFIT SCORECARD RIGHT

		12 100%	13 110%	14 120%	15 130%	16 140%	17 150%
Percent of MARGIN	17.00%						
NET PROFIT @ Standard Performance NET PROFIT from UNSPENT overhead	$7,000	$7,350	$7,700	$8,050	$8,400	$8,750	$8,750
REINVESTMENT Short Term repayment 12 months or less	$875	$919	$963	$1,006	$1,050	$1,094	$1,094
REINVESTMENT Long Term repayment 13 months or more	$875	$919	$963	$1,006	$1,050	$1,094	$1,094
RETAINED EARNINGS - (Tripwire Credit for Receivables)	$875	$919	$963	$1,006	$1,050	$1,094	$1,094
SAVINGS (Safety VALUE)	$875	$919	$963	$1,006	$1,050	$1,094	$1,094
	$3,501						
TAXES (Corporate) - FED (avg only) 17%	$1,190	$1,250	$1,309	$1,369	$1,428	$1,488	$1,488
STATE (avg only) 8%	$560	$588	$616	$644	$672	$700	$700
SHAREHOLDERS Distribution Monthly	$875	$919	$963	$1,006	$1,050	$1,094	$1,094
Additional Distributions (Quarterly OPTIONAL)	$875	$919	$963	$1,006	$1,050	$1,094	$1,094

In the net profit on the right side of normal (column 12), the same rules apply.

NET PROFIT FOR LATER: REINVESTMENT AND RETAINED EARNINGS
Budget Items #8 and #9 of 10

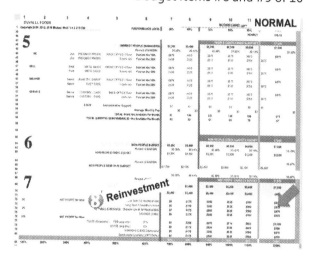

"When and how much can I afford to reinvest into my business, for what?"
"When can I afford to reinvest?"

Built into the Kanketa system is Net Profit for now, and Net Profit for later. There is short term and long-term reinvestments.

Short Term (current) is a one-time reinvestment for anything that the owner expects full repayment of within 12 months.

Long Term (term) is a one-time reinvestment for anything that the owner expects full repayment of within 13 months or more

SHORT-TERM REINVESTMENT

NET PROFIT

REINVESTED
INTO THE BUSINESS
short

Short-term reinvestment implies that whatever Net Profit is being used is fully returned to the owner before the end of the current year. While reinvestment can be for anything, marketing and sales are the focus here since this is the primary use of these funds.

"What should I budget for marketing?"

My answer is in two parts.

First-time marketing Initiative

For any new, first-time marketing initiative such as a website, signage, displays, radio/tv, or the creation of any media, you should not budget more than .0417 (4.17%) of your yearly Normal Margin. If your Margin is $60,000 a month, then your first-time marketing should not exceed $60,000 multiplied by 12 months = $720,00 X .0417 or $30,000 for the year.

Why? Because this is the total amount of Net Profit that you can afford to reinvest to grow your company. I will give you examples in this chapter. If you invest more than this, your company for new marketing projects is out of balance and becomes unsafe.

How do you plan to increase Net Sales this year by 20%? What resources do you need to do this?

Consider your manpower, methods, machines, measurements, milieu (workspace), MTP (most-trusted partner-suppliers), materials, and most importantly of all, the mindset of your team. Do they need coaching and training?

Do you need a new website or marketing media or materials for a market that you are not in yet? Will you need to establish a new line of inventory that is not currently in place?

Your travel budget is not a reinvestment, but an ongoing expense separately treated in your Non-People budget with the exception of a one-time major conference or event.

Monthly marketing maintenance

Additional reoccurring marketing maintenance costs after the first-time marketing initiative are not part of reinvestment. Marketing maintenance is part of your Non-People Fixed cost budget. Marketing maintenance should not exceed .0417 (4.17%) of your Normal Monthly Margin.

In Kanketa, your marketing maintenance is considered a Fixed cost. When your sales are low, you must spend a minimum for marketing to maintain your customer volume. When your sales are high, you must spend a maximum for marketing to grow your business and increase your Normal by 20%. The Retained Earnings part of your profit is designed to support your marketing maintenance effort no matter what condition you are in.

Short-Term Reinvestment
SUMMARY

Budget 12.5% of annual Net Profit at Normal to be used for reinvestment for short-term business growth. Return on investment: 12 months or less.

Types of short term reinvestments:

- Cashflow loan to the business as a line of credit
- First-time marketing initiatives (a website, wearables, radio /tv production, etc.)
- A new hire who is not yet productive
- Purchased inventory that will turn within 12 months
- Payments for a small-asset purchase (printer, office equipment)
- Payments for a one-time start up or set up of office services
- One-time software purchase (accounting software, application software)
- Repaying a short-term bank loan – 12 months or less
- Unexpected, unforeseen short-term opportunities (costs to rescue customers of a competitor who goes out of business)

REINVESTMENTS ARE NOT INTENDED TO PAY FOR MONTHLY FIXED, RECURRING OPERATIONAL EXPENSES.

Kanketa minimum expectations of reinvestment: $3 returned to the owner for every dollar invested

- $1 returns the original dollar that was invested
- $1 returns the profit on the dollar for the risk of the investment
- $1 pays for the owner's time to get involved with the investment (conversations about the re-investment, time to manage the re-investment)

NET PROFIT

REINVESTED
long

As a long-term reinvestment, your monthly payments should not exceed 12.5% of Net Profit at Normal. Any long-term reinvestment into the business is technically always paying the debt as it is incurred. Reinvestment is intended for business growth and not intended for paying back debts.

Ideally, you would plan your reinvestments for the new year once a year within the first week or so when you establish your new budget. Because the new year is based on what you did in the year prior, you already know what your reinvestment budget is and can plan accordingly.

Long-Term Reinvestment
SUMMARY

Budget 12.5% of annual Net Profit at Normal to be used for reinvestment for long-term business growth. Return on investment: 13 months or more.

Types of long-term reinvestment:

- Payments (principal only) for a large asset purchase (vehicle or large equipment)
- Amortized payments to pave a driveway, repair a roof
- Invest in another business
- Payments for long-term financing (SBA 10 year term loan, etc.)

REINVESTMENTS DO NOT PAY FOR MONTHLY FIXED, RECURRING OPERATIONAL EXPENSES
(Monthly long-term leases are in Non-People Fixed Costs.)

NET PROFIT
AS RETAINED EARNINGS
(Savings)

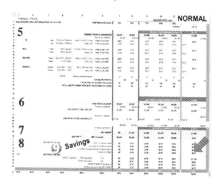

"What should I pay toward debt reduction?"

Retained Earnings is money kept in the company and not disbursed. Kanketa puts aside short-term and long-term money into savings to ensure business safety in the event of an unforeseen situation (positive or negative).

"How much debt can I afford to have?"

Let's take a hard look at debt.

Goal of debt reduction:
Reduce your debt to be equal to or less than NORMAL MONTHLY MARGIN.

How much credit do you plan to allow for call customers combined? Many larger customers will try to make you their bank. But banking your customers is not the business you are in.

Make your policies known to all customers and hold the line. You aren't their bank.

If they try to bully you, simply factor them and charge the interest back. (Factoring is covered later. See section on factoring.) If you don't do this, you will have cashflow problems.

There are three unsafe conditions that Retained Earnings are designed to cover:

1. Unexpected situations that might interrupt the growth and health of the business, such as an unexpected competitor move, an unforeseen change in the marketplace, i.e. a social, technological, economic, environmental, political, ethical or demographic change that could interrupt the business quickly, etc.
2. Expected situations such as late customer payments that extend beyond 30 days (credit that you extend to your customers) and bad debts
3. Late bills beyond 30 days due to creditors.

"How much should we allow for accounts receivable?"

"Tripwire Credit" is the maximum credit that you can afford to give to all customers combined. Trip wire credit is your point of putting your customers on credit hold before using your company's safety to keep them in balance while they throw you out of balance.

Trip wire credit is half of the annual Retained Earnings budget at Normal.

One approach is to allow 60% of your trip wire credit to all customers combined who pay in more than 30 but within 45 days. These people combined are allowed half of Retained Earnings at Normal times 60%.

The folks who pay later than 45 days, but in less than 60 days, share 25% of your trip wire total. And finally, the real delinquents above 61 days share the final 15%.

True Story: Tripping over the Trip Wire

Ted's distributing business in Pittsburgh sold audio gear, small electronics, recording boards, meters, attenuators, etc. Ted supplied 110 dealers. The company billed $150,000 a month. He had dealers of all sizes. Twelve were large dealers, representing about 65% of his business, 45 mid-sized dealers that were 20% of sales and the rest were small occasional dealers who made up the remaining 15%.

Ted had a 40% Margin of $60,000 a month after Cost of Goods Sold. Ted's business was not in balance. While his Net Profit was typically $15,000 a month, he didn't budget or manage the profit well. He was very reactionary in his spending habits and paid the loudest screaming suppliers first. His large customers were slow to pay, taking 45 to 75 days to pay for orders. Ted was afraid to demand stricter payment terms. As his large customers grew, he kept extending credit to match their growth. Finally his banking relationships became strained and he mortgaged his house, his car and spent part of his son's college fund to fund his inventory.

Ted's accounts receivable were over $230,000 and over half of the receivables slid into 120 to 160 days overdue. Eventually he had to rely on high risk high interest lenders for his inventory. Soon, he found himself doing routine loan and debt consolidations. He was no longer borrowing for inventory. He was always borrowing to pay off the previous loans. The interest on his loans became 18%, 20%, 25% and more which exceeded the average 12% Net Profit of the company. Finally, his Net Profit was insufficient to keep up with the loans and he had to get investors. After nine years of being in his own business, he ended up working as employee for the investors, who later sold the company. Ted was laid off.

Had Ted's monthly total loan payments for inventory not exceeded 12.5% of his Net Profit for all customers combined (the same as .0417 % X $60,000 - his monthly Margin at Normal - X 12 months), his business would have grown at the same rate as his customers. He should also have factored the receivables, and charged his customers the factoring interest in the price.

Short-Term Retained Earnings
SUMMARY

NET PROFIT

RETAINED EARNINGS
short

1/8 of Net Profit
TO FACTOR
TRIPWIRE CREDIT

RETAINED EARNINGS – Short

Budget 12.5% of annual Net Profit at Normal to be deposited into savings for short-term business stability - 12 months or less.

Types of savings purposes:

- Credit to customers who are slow payers. Pays for factoring costs.
- Funds receivables 31-89 days.
- Supports unexpected short-term dip in sales.
- Unexpected, unforeseen short-term changes to your company (absenteeism due to employee health issues, small damages to property, etc.)

RETAINED EARNINGS AND SAVINGS ARE NOT USED FOR MONTHLY RECURRING OPERATIONAL EXPENSES.

Long-Term Retained Earnings
SUMMARY

NET PROFIT

RETAINED EARNINGS
long

Budget 12.5% of annual Net Profit at Normal to be deposited into savings for long-term business stability - 12 months or less.

Reasons For Saving:

- Bad debts
- Unexpected, unforeseen changes in the industry that need immediate response, i.e. competitor moves, product obsolescence, vendors or customers going out of business, etc.
- Social, technological, environmental, economic, political legal, ethical and demographic changes of age, education and income changes.
- Unexpected, unforeseen long-term changes to your company (death, incapacitation, disability, permanent absenteeism, large damages to property, etc.)
- Exit of the owner.

    May also be used for general debt reduction

RETAINED EARNINGS AND SAVINGS ARE NOT USED FOR MONTHLY RECURRING OPERATIONAL EXPENSES.

NET PROFIT FOR NOW

CORPORATE TAXES
AND SHAREHOLDERS

America is the only place in the world where it takes more brains to make out the income tax return than it does to make the income. Here are some simple, safe ways to monitor and manage corporate Taxes.

"What should I save for Corporate Taxes?"

These are corporate Taxes for Taxable types of companies such as a C Corporation. These are also saved for taxes of owners of Sub-S corporations, Limited Liability Partnerships, and sole proprietors.

Net Profit For Now

Each month, a diligent business owner should routinely put 25% of the month's Net Profit away for year-end Corporate Taxes (state and federal). Certainly, whatever taxes are not due at the end of the year are returned to the owner.

Safely, I suggest that you save 17% of your Net Profit for federal Corporate Tax and 8% for state Corporate Tax for 25% of your Net Profit total.

Do not use this budget to pay back taxes. Delinquencies, tax penalties and interest on Taxes are paid out of debt payments from long-term Retained Earnings. If your state does not charge Corporate Tax, save it anyway. There are plenty of reasons for this and ways to use this money to reduce your Tax liability overall.

Taxes are based on supply and demand. The government demands, and we supply. The Kanketa "Quadra-Structure," offers many ways to legally control and avoid some of these taxes. For now, these guidelines are sufficient. They are safe amounts for any accountant.

You might find it quite advantageous to expand your business when your state Corporate Taxes are more than $1,700 a year. There are significant tax advantages for this type of expansion. For information on this, submit your request to info@Kanketa.com.

TAX MANAGEMENT

Every business owner falls into two categories of tax management: RESOLUTION and REDUCTION

For decades I have <u>always</u> found every tax return to be in at least one, if not several, of the following conditions:

- OVERPAID

The Taxpayer followed some software instructions and paid accordingly because "it said so." The evidence is right there on the screen. Certainly, that can't be wrong. It instructs millions of users (Quickbooks, TurboTax, Quicken, H&R Block, Tax Act, etc.).

These software systems aren't wrong. They are designed to correctly push volumes of "patients" through the tax hoop. It's no different than the medical profession.

Two over-the-counter pills in a 95-pound person over the age of 12 produces an overdose while a 300 lb. 70-year-old has minimal results as the condition persists.

- INCORRECT

There are always errors in returns of people who do it themselves. Wrong numbers in right places, or right numbers in wrong places all add up to the same thing.

- INACCURATE

With 9 million words in the U.S. tax code (7 bibles) and 20% of the them changing every year, nearly every tax return is inaccurately calculated. Business owners just want to get it off their plate.

- MISGUIDED

Everyone has their favorite accountant who makes them feel safe and secure. And every accountant is trained to fill out government forms and give tax advice. The problem becomes the significant limitation in the training offered. While everyone must do file-your-taxes 101, there are several levels of accounting certifications and licenses available to bookkeepers, accountants, tax attorneys, certified public accountants, etc. They will each guide you to their corner for a fee.

- UNJUSTLY TREATED

The overwhelmed IRS collection agency is processing what comes and computers are doing the processing. There is a high percentage of administrative processing errors that will not be addressed unless the taxpayer is able to find it, understand it, and bring it to someone's attention in a way that makes sense to the agent on the phone within their three-minute conversation allowance.

- MISHANDLED

Professional tax preparers are human. They do guesswork and are often guilty of not following through. The Taxpayer who is pinched between a negligent tax preparer and the stubborn IRS always loses. It often takes years and money to straighten out the smallest mishandled mistakes of a negligent tax preparer.

- UNFILED

Too busy (or too afraid) to file are not acceptable excuses to the IRS as you already know. So, you remain frozen in your tracks and frustrated because your limbs don't move to act.

The Bottom Line to Tax Resolution:
Your business is most likely in one or more of these scenarios today. You don't know who to trust, you don't know why you should trust anyone, and you don't know what you need in the first place.

Am I reasonably close here?

RESOLUTION before REDUCTION (Tax Elimination)

The first request we make to anyone regarding their tax situation is to see their most recently filed tax return. This is the starting point and the current situation

In my experience, the most highly trained, highly experienced professionals to assist in tax resolution are licensed enrolled agents (EA) for the IRS. Their license and position allow them certain privileges that CPAs and other tax practitioners do not have.

What to do with your past tax filings

Have an Enrolled Agent (EA) review your most recently filed tax return to assess any inequities. They should always find oversights and errors and can efficiently correct overpayments and issues of the past with amended tax returns. They can resolve all issues directly with the IRS. There is no need for you to be present. Any fees they might charge will always be much less than the money that they are able to recover.

REDUCTION (Tax Avoidance)

The IRS train doesn't stop. The next biggest business expense after Cost of Goods Sold is taxes. Untreated taxes can rob you of over one-third of your income. Therefore, you should be attentive to your tax situation.

From the moment that your last tax return was filed, your tax responsibilities continue. Under newly formed tax laws each year, your taxes will continue to mount. Starting with your next tax return you are subject to all the same problems mentioned.

Now that you are in the world of tax REDUCTION (during the time that your previous taxes are being handled), everything after that is your current Tax position for upcoming filings.

What will you need for you unfiled tax returns?

- ACCURATE BANK STATEMENTS

Nothing can be filed until you have correct numbers to work with. This is accomplished with reconciled bank statements for EACH MONTH following the last Tax return filed. Without reconciled bank statements, the tax specialists don't know what the deductible expenses are. Month-by-month, errors will pile on top of errors until your books are so twisted, they become unusable.

- TAX REDUCTION HAPPENS MONTHLY (Not at the end of the year)

The tax laws constantly change. The every day-to-day business decisions that you make affect your taxes in some way. Therefore, constant (monthly) auditing is the best practice. Just one good sales month can change everything.

The outcome of monthly monitoring with an EA is paying the least taxes by law while remaining completely compliant. A monthly or quarterly EA review is a low-cost yearly IRS insurance policy that every business should have.

IRS Compliance Insurance

If you want to carry IRS insurance, $285 a month on the average is the cheapest insurance you can have to ensure total freedom from IRS problems.

- EXCELLENT ACCOUNTING PRACTICES MAKE TAX REDUCTION EASIER

Your accountant provides you with a P&L statement that should accurately verify your actual expenses against your budget. Your P&L should show you the details of your Fixed and Semi-Variable expenses and will be the biggest help toward keeping your company balanced.

By comparing your detailed expenses with your budget, you will be able to define, identify, locate, and qualify problems and request solutions from your Tax Specialist for upcoming and existing performance problems as they occur. Don't wait until the end of the month to see how bad things turned out.

RESOLUTION is legal tax recovery. REDUCTION is legal tax avoidance.

NET PROFIT FOR SHAREHOLDERS
OWNER NET INCOME
Budget Item #10 of 10

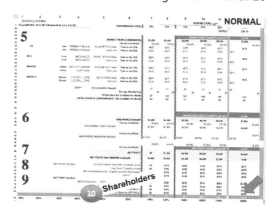

"What should I pay myself?"

If you are striving for financial balance, this answer is very specific. You've seen this before, but it is important enough to repeat.

A Fixed monthly salary as a Workroom manager:

Once a month, (preferably by the 10th) the owner working in the business should receive a specific FIXED monthly salary equal to **4.17%** of the company's monthly Margin at Normal balanced operating levels.

Example: If the monthly Normal Margin is $95,000 the owner's Taxable Fixed monthly salary on the 10th of the month at 4.17% will be **$3,962**.

Semi-Variable performance bonus for the owner as a Workroom manager:

Once a month, (preferably by the 20th), the owner working in the business as a Workroom manager should receive a specific SEMI-VARIABLE monthly bonus of **4.17%** of the company's Margin of the previous month at various operating levels. The management team will always be working one month behind its compensation budget.

Margin multiplied by 4.17% at Normal is the monthly Fixed base salary to maintain the manager's department paid before the 15th of the month **plus 4.17% of Margin multiplied by the month's performance percentage of Normal** as monthly Performance Compensation to grow the owner-manager's department paid before the 20th.

A CLOSER LOOK AT OWNER'S NET PROFIT

"How much should I pay myself as owner?"

There are many ways that an owner of a company makes a Net Profit in their business. A safe profit distribution to the owner is 25% of monthly Net Profit. Whether Net Profit is distributed monthly, quarterly, biannually or annually, this is the number that the owner should count on.

The owner will have more Net Profit than this from various cost savings along the way; but, I suggest that the Scorecard Net Profit for Shareholders is the maximum distributed each month. Distribute the balance quarterly, semi-annually or at the year end. In Chapter 12, Step 10, I will outline four other sources of Net Profit.

OWNER NET PROFIT in addition to Fixed and Semi-Variable compensation:

Once a month by the 10th the owner should receive a Net Profit monthly distribution based on the company's previous monthly Margin. Using the same example:

> If the previous monthly Margin is **100%** of budget or greater: (example: $95,000 or above), the owner's Net Profit on the 10th of the current month will be **8.0%** of Margin or **$7,917 plus Breakage, plus 3 contributions from money saved.**

> If the previous monthly Margin is **90%-99%** of budget: (example: $85,500 - $94,999), the owner's Net Profit on the 10th of the current month will be **7.4%** of Margin or **$6,333.**

> If the previous monthly Margin is **80%-89%** of budget: (example: $76,000 - $85,499), the owner's Net Profit on the 10th of the current month will be **6.3%** of Margin or **$4,750 plus.**

> If the previous monthly Margin is **70%-79%** of budget: (example: $66,500 - $75,999), the owner's Net Profit on the 10th of the current month will be **4.8%** of Margin or **$3,167.**

> If the previous monthly Margin is **60%-69%** of budget: (example: $57,000 - $66,499), the owner's Net Profit on the 10th of the current month will be **2.8%** of Margin or **$1,583.**

> If the previous monthly Margin is **50%-59%** of budget: (example: $47,500 - $56,999), there is **0 Net Profit.**

The owner should not personally pay **any** business bills for any reason. The budgeted Net Profit is strictly intended as the owner's personal funds.

Best method of payment:

Direct deposit to owner and all employees. Don't use paper checks if you can help it.

	7	8	9	10	11	
NET PROFIT @ Standard Performance	$0	$1,400	$2,800	$4,200	$5,600	$7,000
NET PROFIT from UNSPENT overhead	#REF!	#REF!	#REF!	#REF!	#REF!	#REF!
REINVESTMENT Short Term repayment 12 months or less	$0	$175	$350	$525	$700	$875
REINVESTMENT Long Term repayment 13 months or more	$0	$175	$350	$525	$700	$875
RETAINED EARNINGS - (Tripwire Credit for Receivables)	$0	$175	$350	$525	$700	$875
SAVINGS (Safety)	$0	$175	$350	$525	$700	$875
$E VALUE)						$3,501
TAXES (Corporate) - FED (avg only) 17%	$0	$238	$476	$714	$952	$1,190
STATE (avg only) 8%	$0	$112	$224	$336	$448	$560
SHAREHOLDERS Distribution Monthly	$0	$175	$350	$525	$700	$875
Additional Distributions (Quarterly OPTIONAL)	$0	$175	$350	$525	$700	$875

Suppose a balanced company pays $7,000 to People salaries (Fixed and Semi-Variable), $7,000 to Non-People Overhead (Fixed and Semi-Variable), and the owner has a Net Profit of 7,000. Net Profit has four equal parts:

1. In this case the Net Profit would break down into $1,750 for Reinvestment

2. $1,750 for Retained Earnings which is savings

3. $1,750 for taxes

4. And $1,750 for the owner-Shareholder(s) for the month.

This is a safe, Balanced Budget because Fixed Costs equal Semi-Variable Costs equal Net Profit.

It is always interesting to see how outsiders view business owners.

They might see a fancy car, a big house, extended vacations and so on. But they do not see all the trials, tribulations and years of stress, guesswork, the sleepless nights, and the dedication and hard work it took to get there.

Very few People understand that the owner-Shareholders of a safe, balanced company will only keep about 25% of the Net Profit until the company is at or above Normal.

Rationale for the owner to only take 25% of Net Profit monthly.

Owner-Shareholders can be paid at any time up to the budgeted amount. However, consider that Shareholder money might be more flexible than the other budget items.

The Shareholder can earn 18% to 22% per year return on Reinvestment (consistently a lot more than the stock market) by loaning Shareholder money back to the company for cash flow purposes at an acceptable interest of 1.5% per month.

This opportunity will all depend upon the individual financial condition of the Shareholders.

One approach:

Budget 12.5% of total Net Profit paid monthly – to be divided between Shareholders who **DO** need all their money immediately (monthly dividends).

Budget 12.5% of total Net Profit paid monthly – to be divided between Shareholders who **DO NOT** need all of their money immediately (quarterly, biannual or annual dividends).

The use of profit and the distribution of dividends among Shareholders is personal. Kanketa does not make suggestions for how Shareholders distribute or manage their personal money.

Shareholder Dividends

SUMMARY

Kanketa suggests that Shareholder profit distributions work in the same in the same way in short as well as long-term cycles.

If an owner is working as Business Leader and/or as an employee in one or more of the Workrooms in the House of Value, the owner should have sufficient money to meet personal expenses while working IN the business. If the owner is working in the business and the Workroom salary is insufficient to meet daily needs, the owner should write themselves two payments at each pay period.

Payment #1 is the maximum allowed Workroom salary or performance compensation budgeted in order to maintain balance.
Payment #2 is the supplemental income from Net Profit as needed.

One reason why the owner might not take all of the profit as a distribution every month, instead of taking a partial quarterly or annual dividend is for when the business might need additional funding for an unexpected opportunity that could arise to grow the company in the long term – such as opening a new office or simply showing a bank that the company has immediately usable safety funds.

Oh yes, by the way. If you are trying to build a Scorecard by yourself instead of getting a free one from Kanketa, then I will remind you to be very careful of one small detail.

DO NOT RELY ON the NET PROFIT in each PERFORMANCE COLUMN TO FOLLOW THE SAME PERCENTAGE OF NORMAL NET PROFIT.

In other words, Net Profit at 80% performance is not 80% of 100% NORMAL like the MARGIN is.

YOU MUST SUBTRACT YOUR PEOPLE AND NON-PEOPLE COSTS IN EACH PERFORMANCE COLUMN to get the Net Profit in that column.

Recovering from the

ZONES OF RECOVERY

and INDIFFERENCE

"What happens if I have a terrible sales month?"

KANKETA SCORECARD LEFT SIDE – THE ZONE OF RECOVERY

TWO CONSECUTIVE MONTHS under 70% Performance:

What might be happening:

- Market shifts in the need for your products, services
- Uncontrollable external factors, i.e., social, technological, economic, environmental, political, legal, ethical, and/or demographic changes of age, education and income
- Unexpected competitive moves
- Declining product value and product demand

Potential financial problems:

- Cashflow issues
- Reduction in employee wages. Demotivation.
- Reduced budget for operating expenses
- Reduced Reinvestment
- Reduced Retained Earnings
- Reduced Shareholder dividends

At 140% or more, the Kanketa attitude becomes indifferent because this performance usually isn't sustainable and shouldn't be trusted without a lot more evidence of continuous repeatability.

TWO CONSECUTIVE MONTHS over 140% Performance:

What might be happening:

- Product value and product demand has escalated to a new category or level of need
- Competitor might be failing
- You are solving a broken or overlooked process

Potential financial problems:

- Cash drain trying to respond to a new level of growth – cash-flow issues

Exert caution in both cases.

Suggestions until the condition stabilizes.

1. Only spend in a week the amount equal to what was deposited the week before.
2. Cautious spending all around. Do not exceed your allowed budget under any circumstances.
3. Seek assistance from a coach or financial expert. You may contact Kanketa for no-cost guidance during this time.

The BUSINESS OWNER manages all Net Profit – in other words, the bottom line.

It is the BUSINESS LEADER's responsibility to manage all income and expenses above the bottom line

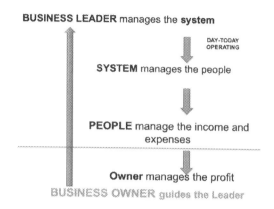

by managing the SYSTEM,
which manages the people,
who manage the expenses at the current performance level,
and are hired to give the owner the Net Profit to manage.

"How do I Manage Multiple Locations?"

The answer is simple. Have a separate Budget and Scorecard for each location. Don't mix budgets, scorecards and locations.

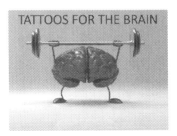

THREE SCORECARD TATTOOS FOR THE BRAIN

Now, let's walk away with three main ideas from Score carding.

#1 Breakage is your hidden money every month between performance levels. Put it into savings. You can't save enough.

#2 Reduce your debt to be equal to or less than NORMAL MONTHLY MARGIN

#3 Protect the safety of your company by maintaining Tripwire Credit limits.

CHAPTER 12:

PUTTING IT ALL TOGETHER

Money In

Money Out

Money Kept

Money Managed

31 CONCEPTS OF A

HIGH PERFORMING COMPANY

"WHY DO MY STARTUPS KEEP FAILING?"
This Chapter offers a good start for this question.
The entire picture is found on page 220.
Do these, and you won't keep failing.

WHAT YOU HAVE LEARNED
IN A NUTSHELL ...

Real Answers To 31 Money Questions That Keep Business Owners Up At Night
At the core of each question are main ideas; "Tattoos for the Brain" that will help a small business owner to understand the fundamentals of a high performing company.

Concept 1: The 30 day Company
The owner of a high performing company pays all its bills within 30 days by isolating and managing their business one month at a time. The business restarts at midnight on the first day of every month and ends at 11:59 p.m. on the last day of the month. During that time, the business either made or lost money. Everything outside of the immediate 30-day cycle is irrelevant.

Concept 2: The Problem With GAAP Accounting

GAAP was invented for Tax compliance purposes, but it is almost useless for small business decision-making. The expense categories in the GAAP system are usually arranged alphabetically according to expense types: Advertising, Bank fees, Cleaning service, Delivery, etc. Alphabetical order is almost useless for helping small business owners make good day-to-day decisions.

Concept 3: Business Financial Advisor vs. Accountant

A high performing company relies on two Advisors. Each provide different services.

BUSINESS ADVISOR	ACCOUNTANT
✓ THE FUNNEL - pours the splash	✓ THE SPOUT - channels the drips
✓ BIG PICTURE	✓ DETAILS, REFINEMENT
✓ The SHOE...	✓ ... The LACES
✓ MAIN CATEGORIES	✓ SUB-CATEGORIES
✓ BIG SWIPES	✓ TRIM and CLEAN UP
✓ CREATES BALANCE	✓ MAINTAINS BALANCE
✓ DESIGNS, DEVELOPS, IMPLEMENTS BALANCE	✓ MANAGES BALANCE
✓ PROACTIVE	✓ AVOIDS REACTIVE
✓ MONTHLY REPORTS	✓ QUARTERLY REPORTS
✓ LEAD – Front end	✓ FOLLOW – Back end
✓ QUANTIFIES	✓ VERIFIES
✓ BUDGET, SCORECARD	✓ P&L, BALANCE SHEET

Concept 4: There Are Ten Parts To A Kanketa Balanced Budget

These are 10 numbers to always know about your business. The goal is to create balance within these categories.

Money In:
1. Gross Sales 2. Net Sales 3. Cost of Quality

Money Out:
4. Cost of Goods Sold, 5. Fixed Costs, 6. Semi-Variable Costs

Money Kept
7. Reinvestment, 8. Retained Earnings

Money Managed
9. Taxes, 10. Shareholder Distribution

Concept 5: A Company of One

The owner in a company of one must market, sell, conduct customer service, and be sure that customers don't leave. When s/he is not doing these things, s/he is creating products, dealing with suppliers, attending to operational responsibilities, and doing bookkeeping. The workload of a business is in proportion to the number of managers available. None of these responsibilities can be ignored or the rest become crippled.

Concept 6: Financial Balance

Kanketa defines Financial Balance as... the point in the Margin at which Fixed Overhead costs, the Semi-Variable Overhead costs, and the Net Profit are equal. Financial Balance is created from all money in a business, repositioned differently.

Kanketa defines Normal as... an ideal monthly performance level, based on the 12-month average of income and expenses from the previous tax year, in which all resources of the company are fully utilized. Normal is the center of a business's financial universe and the starting point for company growth.

Gross Sales

Gross Sales are the total collected amount that you invoice before the Cost of Quality (discounts, rework, returns, samples, free assessments, warranties and error). A net sale is the amount of money you have to work with after discounts, returns, allowances, and error. At one point, someone came up with the idea of labeling all the aspects of profit and loss with a set of numbers called "account codes." There are account codes for every type of business. The category of Gross Revenue does not necessarily specify which money you earn comes from the sales of your products and services. It is crucial to keep income and expenses carefully identified. The use of account codes throughout your financial management system will help.

The Sale

In Kanketa, a sale must be fully earned, and is only final when there is nothing more to deliver and no further liability. By law, you may only spend "earned income" from customer payments that you receive in proportion to the work for which you have evidence of satisfactory completion. "Accrual" is the accumulation of payments or benefits owed to you by a customer for work that has been completed, but not yet invoiced. Accrual is an accounting method that records revenues and expenses when they are incurred, regardless of when cash is exchanged.

Net Sales After the Cost of Quality

A Net Sale, not Gross Sale, is the primary income number that is used to determine the performance of a business. A Net Sale is the result of total deposits for products and services, minus the Cost of Quality. The Cost of Quality should be monitored, tracked, and be ultimately recoverable in the price of the products and services.

Cost of Goods Sold

If you don't have a job, you don't have Cost of Goods Sold. Your balance of Cost of Goods Sold to Gross Sales is a safety factor. The lower the Cost of Goods percent of Gross Sales, the higher the percentage of business safety. Nothing is a Cost of Goods Sold unless there is a customer who buys it and there is a verifiable job. No job? No Cost of Goods Sold. The lower the Cost of Goods percent to Gross Sales, the higher the percentage of business safety that exists. The goal of Cost of Goods Sold is to balance and market like- product types so the percentage of Cost of Goods Sold to Net Sales is relatively constant from year to year.

Margin

Margin isn't everything. It's the only thing. Margin, not Gross Sales, determines real growth of the business. In Kanketa, the budgeted Margin at 100% Normal has six equally balanced parts.

1. Fixed People Costs (managers' salaries)
2. Fixed Non-People Costs (month-to-month, predictably repeatable overhead expenses necessary to maintain business performance and profitability: All Fixed overhead costs that aren't manager salaries - rent, insurance, recurring monthly contracts, etc.)
3. Semi-Variable People Costs (managers' compensation that changes month to month with performance)
4. Semi-Variable Non-People Costs (changing monthly overhead expenses necessary to grow the business and increase profitability – gas, utilities, office supplies, etc.)
5. Owner Net Profit For Later

6. Owner Net Profit For Now
When all these budget components are equal, you have a Balanced Budget.

Breakeven

When your Kanketa Balanced Performance Budget **is at exactly 50%** of Normal (not 51%), you are at breakeven.

Margin percent of Net Sales at Normal parallels sales performance.
Margin is the only indicator of the growth of a business.
Net Profit is in the Margin and is only zero at exactly 50% of Normal Performance.
Debt is paid from Net Profit.

Concept 7:

There Are Two Types of Margin: Equalized Margin and Balanced Margin

People Costs pay for your managers. Non-People Costs are your overhead operating expenses. Fixed Costs do not change monthly by more than 5%. Semi-Variable Costs do change monthly in 10% performance increments based on prior month's sales performance. .

The Kanketa House of Value

In Kanketa, every manager contributes and is compensated on equal terms, compensation and benefits..

Concept 8: Workrooms and Corridors

The back office on the left side of the House of Value is comprised of the MAKE and DELIVER Workrooms. In the front office, there are the SELL and SERVICE Workrooms. The front office deals with the marketplace and the external customers. The back office serves and treats the front office as their internal customers. Each Workroom manager has two primary responsibilities.

Concept 9: Responsibilities of Workroom Managers

Marketing
must maintain Normal sales volume dollar value of new, first-time prospect opportunities.

Sales
must convert marketing opportunities into first-time customer payments (contracts sold).

Customer Service
must ensure that all customers are fully satisfied with every transaction – error-free.

Customer Care
must ensure that 80% of Normal sales volume of first- time customers become continuous, annually repeating opportunities.

Product Management
must design the product or service profitably, with all purchasing done at a supplier cost that guarantees profitability.

Production
must produce the product within budget – error-free.

Velocity
Must deliver job volume satisfactorily – on time.

Self-Directed Leadership
must maintain employee productivity and employee engagement within the allowed People compensation budgets.

Concept 10: People Costs: Manager Salaries
Pay managers half of their total compensation for maintaining their Workroom performance, and the rest as semi-variable compensation for increasing their Workroom performance. Give raises once a year to everyone on the management team based on the prior year's performance.

Concept 11: Semi-Variable Costs in The Margin: Non-People Overhead
The monthly budget follows sales performance and increases or decreases from the 100% Normal performance column in 10% increments based on the prior month's performance. When sales are higher than Normal, you put more gas in your car to service customers. When your sales are lower than Normal, you use less gas to service customers. When your sales are higher

than Normal, you use more postage, more office supplies, more electricity. Semi-variable cost items can change from year to year, but the 16.67% semi-variable performance budget percent of the Margin remains constant.

Concept 12: Overspent, Unspent. When Costs Don't Fit the Budget

When the actual Fixed Costs or Semi-Variable Costs exceed their budget, the budget will show a negative overage as a line item. If any budget is overspent, the company is not balanced and is losing critical profit.

Concept 13: Unspent Margin: Budget is Equal To Fixed Plus Semi-Variable Expenses

It will be rare that Fixed Costs exactly equal Semi-Variable Costs. One will almost always exceed the other. When either fixed or semi-variable budgets have money left over after all expenses are paid, the budgets are underspent. The unspent money is available at any moment for unexpected changes that might occur within the current year. This is handled by simply adding an additional "Unspent" line to each budget. Unspent money is deposited into Savings.

Concept 14: Fix it. Don't Mix it

Never pay for an overspent (negative) part of the budget on one side of the budget with unspent money from the other side. Always work to adjust the budgets to be equal.

Concept 15: Components of Kanketa Net Profit

- 12.5% Reinvestment Short Term
- 12.5% Reinvestment Long Term
- 12.5% Retained Earnings Short Term
- 12.5% Retained Earnings Long Term
- 17% Corporate Tax – Federal
- 8% Corporate Tax – State
- 12.5% Owner-Shareholder Distribution quarterly, biannually, and/ or annually
  There is Net Profit for later, and Net Profit for now.

12.5% Short-term Reinvestment – 12 months or less is the expected timeframe that the return on investment should come back to the owner

12.5% Long-term Reinvestment – 13 months or more is the expected timeframe that the return on investment should come back to the owner

12.5% Short-term Retained Earnings –-12 months or less is the expected timeframe that the profit is used to support potential business problems, such as bad debts and business interruptions.

12.5% Long-term Retained Earnings - 13 months or more is the expected timeframe that the profit is used to support unforeseen emergencies.

25% Short-term Tax Payments - 12 months or less. The Net Profit from each month builds the Corporate Tax savings account. On the average, save 17% of Net Profit for federal Corporate Tax. On the average, save 8% of Net Profit for state Corporate Tax.

Concept 16: Shareholder Disbursements

12.5% Monthly Shareholder Disbursements – pays shareholders for the previous month based on performance.

12.5% Quarterly Distribution to Shareholders is a suggested

Concept 17: Scorecard Layout

The Scorecard displays monthly business performance at a glance. The 100% Normal Balanced Budget is at the center. The business performance in the previous month determines the budget column of the Scorecard in the new month. There are five columns to the left of Normal, and five columns to the right. The 100% Normal column in the center is your average column from which all other columns are calculated. One-third of Normal is Fixed Cost, one-third of Normal is Semi-Variable cost. One-third Net Profit only occurs at Normal.

Only at Normal do the total of People Fixed Costs plus Non-People fixed cost (spent and unspent) equal the total of People Semi-Variable Costs plus Non-People Semi-Variable Costs. They each equal the Net Profit. The 100% Normal performance column is the only place on the Scorecard that this balance occurs.

Concept 18: Breakage

Breakage is the additional Net Sales generated between the current month and the next performance column from the previous months performance after the month's budgeted Cost of Quality and Cost of Goods Sold have been deducted.

Concept 19: Value of the Business Owner's Time

Divide your last year's Taxable income by 1,000 to get your hourly value as the owner of your business. Up to 1,000 hours a year is what the owner has available to work IN the business. The other 1,000 hours is what the owner has available to work ON the business.

Concept 20: Necessary Line of Credit is Normal Monthly Margin (NMM) multiplied by 1.8. This is the maximum amount of money needed to operate your company every month without additional funding.

Concept 21: Business Checkbook Balances

Normal Monthly Margin multiplied by .67 is the amount of money that should be in your Fixed and Semi-Variable account combined at all times to cover one month of operational expenses.

Concept 22: Goal for the Savings Account

Normal Monthly Margin X 4 X .67 is the ideal amount of money needed to keep the company safe from unexpected turbulence.

Concept 23: Maximum Credit Allowed to All Customer Combined Without Charging Interest:

Half of one month of Normal Monthly Margin is the maximum amount of credit beyond 30 days that a financially safe company can afford to give to all customers combined.

Concept 24: Goal of Debt Reduction:

Reduce your total debt to be equal to or less than your total NMM Monthly Margin at Normal.

Concept 25: Maximum allowed for accounts receivable before Factoring

Accounts Receivable should not exceed half of the annual Retained Earnings budget at Normal.

Concept 26: Goal of Tax Savings:

Suggested: Save 17% of your Net Profit for federal corporate Tax and 8% for state corporate Tax for 25% of your Net Profit total.

Concept 27: Zone of Recovery when the company is underperforming

Two consecutive months under 70% of Normal Performance

Problem: Cash drain trying to hold the company together – cash flow issues

Concept 28: Zone of Indifference when the company is randomly over performing

Two consecutive months over 140% of Normal Performance that is not planned

Problem: Cash drain trying to respond to a new level of growth – cash flow issues

Concept 29: The Job of a Business Leader

The BUSINESS OWNER manages all Net Profit – in other words, the bottom line.

It is the BUSINESS LEADER's responsibility to manage all income and expenses above the bottom line by managing the SYSTEM, which manages the People, who manage the

expenses at the current performance level, and are hired to give the owner the Net

Concept 30: Organize Your P&L to Match the Budget

Ideally, your P&L should be organized so that you can clearly see the ten main Kanketa budget categories that include every expense in your business.

Concept 31: More Than 20% Annual Sales Growth Over The Prior Year's Normal Is Risky Business.

For clarification, the 20% rule assumes that the company is using its money and resources to the fullest level.

Call For free help in your business with any part of this book:

888-679-4410

IN A WORD

In my professional career I have owned 26 businesses of every size, shape and dimension: manufacturing, business-to-business services, distribution, wholesale, retail, nonprofit, onshore, offshore, in the air, a company of three, and a company of 103. I started companies from scratch, bought them, managed them, sold them, merged and unmerged them, leased them out, partnered in them – you name it.

I have personally applied every instruction in this book. Early on (in the 1960s), I wasn't as skillful with these practices and had limited success. Through decades of constant refinement, I became more confident as I saw the system improve. By the 1990s, the results were reliable and astounding.

The Biggest Problem With a Small Business

It's small. Too many small business owners believe that they are their business. They think that if they go way, their business goes away. "I might as well do it myself. It just won't be done right unless I've got my hands in it. You just can't get good help these days," is a common refrain.

They must touch every product, write every check, and guide every move. They mistrust everything and everyone. Their accountant can't do it right. Suppliers are lurking in every corner, always ready to take them for a ride. Their customers are constantly beating them down on price. Their undeserving competitors are getting all the jobs. All along, their handful of incompetent employees are robbing them blind. And on, and on, and on.

Most of this is simply not true. In hundreds of candid interviews with business owners big and small I've found well-intended, quality-minded, honest, hard-working individuals who are willing to do what it takes to help their customers, vendors and employees grow and be better off. Many are searching for answers. The common thread is they all have good intentions.

To those who believe that they are their business, the reality is that every business is seen by the government as a FEIN number (Federal Employee Identification Number). Every business is a living, breathing entity that is subject to the same operating rules, same Tax laws, same banking regulations, and the same compliance requirements as the next. Al's Bait Shop in every way observes the same rules as Amazon, Google and General Motors. The only difference is how the businesses are managed. **R**

A small company of ten people has the same functional demands as a single department in a medium-size company of a hundred. A medium-size company of a hundred operates functionally like a single department in a large company of thousands. The small company sells to an outside customer. The small department in a large company sells its services to an inside customer. The small business manages a checkbook. The small department in a large company treats a budget like a checkbook. The small owner makes a profit.

The small department in a large company is a profit center that shares in the profit. It's all the same stuff in a different wrapper.

As I have said earlier, there are millions of companies that are doing just fine without Kanketa Financial Balance. You're feeding your family. You're putting the kids through school. You get away now and then. If you have no money problems or frustrations, then again, please, you should toss this book into a shredder. This is about reducing money worries and making your life easier.

There's nothing here to study. Just do the steps. Achieving financial balance is an action plan that you can put into motion immediately to get on track with where you want to be with your money matters.

I hope that you explore this information further and experiment with it in your own business. It might change your life.

It changed mine.

Questions? Need a free Scorecard for your business? Need help with any of this?

Call 888-692-4410, ext. 1.

THE AUTHOR

Since 1965, Mike Wolf served as a speech writer, trainer, executive coach and consultant to CEOs and Senior Management of Global Fortune 1,000 enterprises.

 During his career, he created hundreds of marketing campaigns for U.S. and offshore companies. Mr. Wolf's extensive background across many industries, from manufacturing, to service, retail, trade and non-profits paved the way to KANKETA, "Journey In Balance", a unique, holistic philosophy for operating a small business. Kanketa's proven management methodology is not taught in business schools anywhere. Kanketa helps small business owner achieve personal financial freedom owning their own businesses.

Kanketa is commonly referred to as the Science of Small Business Management.

The mission of Kanketa Global Systems is to transform small businesses with 30 or less employees into high performing companies. The Kanketa system continues to create dramatic results in significantly reduced time frames for small business owners across the globe.

KANKETA
PUBLICATIONS

Kanketa House of Value Series:

Structure, Finance, Product Management, marketing, Sales, Production,
Velocity, Customer Service, Self-Directed Leadership, Customer Care
Business Leadership, Business ownership

Printed in the United States
By Bookmasters